Learner Services

Please return
on or before
the last date
stamped below

CITY COLLEGE
NORWICH

- 7 NOV 2005   0 8 APR 2011

2 8 NOV 2005   2 0 MAY 2013

2 6 JUN 2013

1 7 APR 2007

2 0 MAR 2009   2 9 JUN 2018

2 5 NOV 2009   0 6 JUN 2022

2 3 FEB 2010
1 6 MAR 2010

1 4 MAY 2010

1 1 NOV 2010

A FINE WILL BE CHARGED FOR OVERDUE ITEMS

HUMAN HORIZONS SERIES

ADHD

How to Deal with Very Difficult Children

ALAN TRAIN

A Condor Book
Souvenir Press (E&A) Ltd

First published 1996 by
Souvenir Press (Educational & Academic) Ltd,
43 Great Russell Street, London WC1B 3PA
and simultaneously in Canada

ISBN 0 285 63311 2

Typeset by Rowland Phototypesetting Ltd,
Bury St Edmunds, Suffolk
Printed in Great Britain by
The Guernsey Press Co. Ltd, Guernsey, Channel Islands

To my wife Vivienne and to our children
Jonathan, Peter, Helen and Matthew:
Vincit Qui Patitur! F.G.S.B.

Contents

Part One

UNDERSTANDING THE CHILD
WITH ADHD

1 Transforming Your Child's Behaviour

Do you feel that you can no longer cope with your child's behaviour, that you and his school have done everything possible for him and that he is beyond redemption?

You are most probably mistaken: for years you may have suffered unnecessarily because of your child.

You may have tormented yourself with the thought that his difficult behaviour was the result of your incompetence. Perhaps, after years of genuine endeavour, you have even been driven to conclude that you have given birth to someone who is evil and in your despair have finally decided that your child was born this way and that there is nothing you can do to alter him. You may deeply resent him because his behaviour has turned you into a physical and nervous wreck, destroyed your career or your marriage, caused friends to desert you and neighbours to shun you. In your eyes he may have become the embodiment of everything you hate in yourself and others. In essence, you may feel that he has made your life a misery and that you have had enough.

During all these years of personal suffering you may never have heard of the medical condition which can be the cause of difficult behaviour in children and of the treatment which can bring immediate relief for yourself and hope for your child's future.

You should not feel guilty about this. Many other parents have blamed themselves for the behaviour of their child and have struggled to find a solution on their own. They have defended their child and because of him or her have suffered pain and humiliation. They have experienced the ultimate shame of admitting to themselves that their child is beyond help.

Professionals have not made their lives easier. They have joined in the blame game and been too keen to condemn parents of difficult children as negligent. They have been unable to appreciate the hard work and misery involved in raising such a child. To many teachers, child care workers and social workers, difficult children are simply the product of bad parenting. Little have they appreciated the level of stress which some children place on their families, or understood that some children are difficult from birth and that their temperament is often at the root of much family discord and problematic behaviour in school.

Because of this background of distress and ignorance, I have decided to begin with a story. If you are the parent of a difficult child you will recognise its truth—you may, however, be pleasantly surprised at the outcome; if you are a professional you may need to persuade yourself that the story has any basis in reality. I can assure you that it has. The names of the characters have been altered to maintain confidentiality.

*   *   *

Liz listened to Simon screaming at her from the bottom of the stairs. 'Mum! I want my breakfast! Why are you always in bed? I hate you, you cow!' She heard the sound of a chair scraping hard on the kitchen floor and the clattering of the cupboard doors.

She panicked. Where was she? Was she dreaming? Had she overslept? She felt so very tired.

She struggled to put on her dressing-gown. It was just after six. He had probably been up for a good half-hour already. She stretched and then braced herself. She looked into the mirror, took a deep breath and told herself that she was going to stay calm.

'Bitch!' she heard him say as she walked downstairs. 'I'll kill you, you bitch!' A dish crashed to the floor, smashing into fragments.

She said, 'Simon! Come on now! We'll have less of this! Here, sit down and have these!'

He pulled away from her and then with a surge threw himself forwards, hitting her around her body with his fists and kicking up at her. 'I hate you!' he shouted. 'Why don't you fuck off, you old bitch, you old bag? Why don't you leave me to get my breakfast every day, you buggery bitch?'

Unable to hold him, she backed away and turned her face,

cowering to protect herself as he threw a cup. 'You naughty boy!' she shouted. 'Why do you do this to me? Wait until your father returns. He'll sort you out!'

He leaped onto the table. 'You do it if you're so bloody clever! Come on, let's see how good you are, you bitch! Cow!' He taunted her with a dance. 'Who's a lazy cow then? My mum! Who's a fat bitch? My mum! Fuck! Bloody fuck!' He screamed at the top of his voice.

She was exhausted, hardly awake and he had started. She simply could not face any more of it.

She went for him, knocking him onto the floor with one crazy, unconscious sweep of her arm carrying a massive blow straight through him. It took her off balance and she slumped across the table.

The sudden silence made her panic. He was lying quietly on the tiles, motionless.

Slowly she raised herself from the table and went to kneel beside him. He was so still. Had she finally silenced him for ever? She rubbed her eyes. This was the moment she had always dreaded. Then she heard him quietly mutter 'Bitch. Bloody bitch! Bugger bitch' under his breath and saw his tears. She held him in her arms and wept with relief. Yet again she had come very close to the edge.

When she had stopped her sobbing and said, 'Why do you do it, my love? Why do you hate Mum so much?' he nestled into her, and she knew then that he would be with her for a while. He would stay close like that until he was rested. She would gently carry him to the lounge where she would lay him on the sofa and cover him with his coat. Later he would say he was sorry. This had happened many times before.

At ten o'clock, when she told him they would need to go shopping, he said, 'I'm not going.'

'But, Simon, we must go. I need to get bread, milk and some potatoes. Come on now, get your coat on.'

'I'm not going. I'm going to watch telly.'

'Simon! Get your coat on! You are coming and that's all there is to it! I'm going, and I'm not leaving you here on your own!'

'Bitch!' he shouted as he ran out of the room. 'Make me go, then! I'm not going anywhere!'

'Simon!' she shouted. 'Come here!' He had gone upstairs and was quiet. 'Where are you? Come here right now and get this coat on!' She ran upstairs, stamping her feet as she went, thundering up to him.

He was standing next to the wardrobe in his room. 'All right, Mum. Can I get some sweets?'

She sighed. 'Come on. We'll never get there at this rate.'

They were halfway to the bus stop when he decided to change his mind.

'You must come!' she whispered angrily into his ear.

'Don't want to.'

'Look, when we get there we'll go for something to eat, and then we can get your magazine.'

He raised his voice. 'I don't want anything to eat! I'm not hungry. Silly bitch!'

She looked round. A woman with a small child had stopped and was watching from the other side of the street. A few yards away the milkman had paused and was turned towards them. 'I'll be OK,' she said. She was beginning to shake.

As calmly as she could and holding herself in she said, 'Simon, listen very carefully. If you do not come with me now, this minute, I am going—and I am going whether you come or not!'

He stared across the road.

She walked away from him.

When she had nearly reached the bus stop at the top of the road she could stand it no longer and looked round. At first she could not see him, but then her attention was drawn by the woman with the small child, who was mid-way between them. She had been able to observe what was happening. 'He's there!' she shouted.

Liz stepped off the kerb and looked back to where she had left Simon. He was lying stretched out motionless in the road.

She tried to scream but no sound came. She realised the horror of what he was doing but was unable to move.

She heard the woman shout, 'I'll get him!' and watched with fear and shame as Simon stood up and then calmly walked towards her at the bus stop.

On the bus he insisted on sitting by the window. She was still shaking and trying to contain herself.

He pushed past her.

'Where are you going now?' she asked.

He ignored her.

He spent much of the journey walking to the front window and then to the back, and twice she had to stop him from going downstairs.

When he finally decided to sit back in his place she felt the whole deck of passengers heave a sigh of relief. The bus was crowded with workers and shoppers. They used this journey as a quiet time to charge themselves up for the rest of the day.

He kicked the back of the seat in front.

'Simon!'

After a momentary silence she heard him whisper, just loud enough for the passengers in front to hear, 'Bitch! You fucking bitch! Cunt mother! Beat me up all the time when no one's looking! One day they'll find out! Child molester! Bitch bugger!'

She frowned at him to stop.

He did and said out loud, 'When we get there, can I have those new trainers you promised me?'

She muttered an uncomfortable 'I suppose'. She had not intended to spend that kind of money this month. She felt cornered, unable to say more. Anything else would only have meant further embarrassment.

He sat still for a moment and then squirmed past her.

'Simon! Come here!' But it was too late. He had disappeared down the stairs. When she caught up with him he was hanging off the platform and she decided that they were close enough to town to walk. At the next stop she pulled him off the bus.

'You naughty boy!' she cried. 'Why must you always embarrass me like that?'

She longed to sit down with a coffee somewhere, and although she knew what might happen she decided to take Simon into a McDonald's. He quickly leaped at the chance and was through the door before she had time to see whether there was any room for them. She saw that the café was not very full. Simon had noticed too and was running between the tables shouting, 'Should we have this one or this or this or this!' He knocked a few elbows and turned a few heads. But they were in there now and she felt that she had to make the most of it.

'Come here, Simon, love. Come and sit near the window.'

For once he did as he was told.

'What would you like?' she asked.

He said nothing.

'What would you like, Simon?'

She shook his arm but he was paying no attention. He was looking out of the window and then into the mirror. He stood on his seat and leaped up and down, watching his reflection.

'Simon! Sit down. What would you like?'

He jumped to the floor and was about to sit down again when he noticed a small toy on the floor. It was out of a crisp packet. He stretched under the table trying to reach for it.

'Come here, Simon. Sit up and behave!'

'I want it. It's mine. Let me have it!'

He got away from her as she tried to pull him back.

'Oh!' she gasped. 'I've had enough! Come on!'

She knew that it would be hard to get him out of there but it was better than crucifying herself with embarrassment for the next twenty minutes.

She finally grabbed him and bundled him towards the door. It had gone quiet. People were staring.

'Go on, then, beat me up!' he shouted. 'That's all you do! Bitch! Bitch!' He screamed and dropped to the floor, forcing her to strain as she pulled him with her. It was only the shame and humiliation which gave her the strength to drag him out of the café.

When she finally stopped, shaking and on the verge of tears, she heard him say, 'Sorry, Mum. I really am sorry.'

She would have asked him why he had behaved this way, but she knew that he could not reply: there was no reason and there would be no answer.

They went straight home without bothering to shop for the food, never mind the trainers. She said to herself that she would rather starve than put up with him any longer. She wanted to get him home, out of sight of everyone, and if she had to go out she would just leave him and go.

When they got home he ran to his room and she could hear him banging things about as he searched for something that would amuse him. There was a momentary silence and then he dashed downstairs. He looked around the lounge and ran up again. He turned his cassette player on as loud as he could, and she felt the ceiling vibrate as he jumped up and down on his bed in time to the music.

Five minutes later he was downstairs switching on the television and emptying the contents of the magazine rack on to the carpet in a frantic effort to find the *TV Times*. When he could not find it he jumped up and ran through the kitchen into the back garden. For a brief moment she felt she could relax. She turned the TV off and went upstairs to switch off his radio. There was silence.

After a minute or so she began to panic. He was out of sight and everything was quiet. She knew that this meant danger, that he was in some kind of trouble. She scanned the garden and saw nothing. She hurried upstairs and looked out of the window. She looked to her left where she could see the main road. He was not there. She couldn't see him. Where had he gone?

She ran so quickly she missed half the stairs. Just as she was about to open the front door something made her stop. There was a smell of burning!

She saw his legs first, sticking out from behind the half-closed kitchen door. She shouted, 'Dear God, What have you done!'

But when she peered round the door, fearing the worst, she saw instead a smiling face. 'Look, Mum. I can do it!' He sat surrounded by dead matches, holding one which he had just lit and which he now threw into the air.

'Simon! You must never play with those! It's very dangerous! Give them here!'

'No! Let me have them. I want them. You can't take them. They're mine! Go away, bitch, go away! Let me have them! I want them!' He spat at her, kicked at her and thrust his fist into her face.

'Simon! Stop! Give me those matches!'

She knew what was going to happen and was powerless to prevent it.

She looked at him as he lay still on the kitchen floor. She knelt down by him and held him and he nestled into her. She cried and said she was sorry, she hadn't meant to hit him. She loved him and only wanted him to be a good boy. He sobbed and took deep, irregular breaths. She heard him say, 'I'm sorry too, Mum', and then held him as he drifted into a deep sleep which they had so often shared.

He woke an hour later and rubbed his eyes. She had laid him on the sofa and covered him with his coat.

'Have a drink, love,' she said. She gave him hot chocolate and a biscuit. 'Do you feel better now?'

She switched the television on to watch the six o'clock news.

He said, 'Can I watch *Startrek*?'

She hesitated but she knew she would have to give in. 'All right,' she said, 'I've seen the headlines.'

Two minutes after she had switched over and gone to get herself another cup of tea, she heard him run upstairs. She returned to her seat and flicked back to BBC1.

He came racing down, shouting, 'I knew you'd do that! Why can't I watch *Startrek*? It's not fair, you always get your own way!'

She was tired and let him carry on, but she didn't change channels. He stormed into the kitchen and she heard him banging about in the cupboards.

'Do you want some supper?' she asked, sensing an opportunity to acquire a positive response.

'Bugger off, bitch. Bitch cunt! I don't want anything! Just leave me alone!'

Yet again she had mistimed her approach. From the sound of it he was beginning to throw things about.

'Simon! Come in here and sit down!' She knew that he wouldn't and that she sounded increasingly pathetic. She was tired and consoled herself with the knowledge that there was only an hour or two to go before he went to bed.

She turned the volume up and sank back in her chair. He could do what he wanted. She wasn't going to move.

Tomorrow would bring the same problems. She might as well let him get on with it.

She lost count of the times he ran up and down the stairs, and of the times he turned on his radio. She lost interest in his shouting and swearing. She found herself apologising to him for being a poor mother. She said he could stay up till midnight if he wished because she only wanted him to be happy. That was all she wanted—peace and happiness. Nothing else. Exhausted, annihilated, she fell asleep before he did. Only when she heard an enormous crash did she wake and realise that he was still up.

'Simon! Get to bed! Right now!' She was too tired to find out what he had smashed, and made her way slowly towards her bedroom. He had sensed the urgency in her voice, and at one hour past midnight was himself beginning to feel drowsy. He climbed into bed and pulled the duvet tight over his head. His knees came up to his chest and he comforted himself by sucking his thumb. His day had lasted nineteen hours and in five hours' time he would be stirring again, recharged and ready to go.

The following morning at about seven o'clock, when he had already been scurrying about the house for an hour or so, he banged on her bedroom door and jumped on the bed beside her. He pulled the cover from her face. 'Mum. I want my breakfast. Come on! Get up! I'm hungry!'

He leaped off the bed and fiddled with her hairbrush. He was quiet for a moment as he wound up her lipstick and amused himself by drawing with it on the mirror, but he soon leaped back on top of her and gritted his teeth. 'Muuum! I want my breakfast! Get up! Come on! Get up!'

She didn't move.

'Cow face!'

She was still. Motionless. 'Simon, I . . .'

'I want my breakfast, Mum. Come on. Get up!'

She looked through him, and he sensed that she was different. He stopped moving.

'Mum. Mum. What's wrong, Mum?' He touched her hand. 'Come on. Get up . . .'

But she lay there, empty and exhausted, unable to do more than whisper a few words: 'Go and get Maggie from next door . . . just go and get Maggie.'

Maggie realised what had happened. 'It's all been too much for you, Liz. You can't be expected to carry on like this. You've had this since he was born. He's killing you. I don't know how many times I have to tell you. You're a fool. He needs more help than you can ever give him. He needs to be away somewhere. He'll finish you off one day if he hasn't already. You look absolutely dreadful. I'm going to call the doctor.'

'No, Maggie . . . I don't want to . . .' But she was too weak to do anything about it.

Maggie took Simon with her. 'Just you rest,' she said. 'The doctor will be here mid-morning.'

Liz told the doctor that she felt numb. It was nothing to do with her body, she just felt numb, dead, inside. Before him Dr Good saw a young woman of thirty-one who looked at least ten years older. Her face was gaunt. Her eyes, red and weak, looked anywhere but into his. Without examining her he could see bruises on her arms.

'Tell me about it,' he said.

Fearing that her eight-year-old son would be taken from her, she resisted.

'Mrs Jones,' the doctor said, 'I know what's been going on. Your neighbour told me. She's worried, you know. Come on, it's time for the truth.'

He stayed for over half an hour, listening to her every word. When he left she sensed that he had heard and understood. She was comforted by his reassurance that there was a solution to her years of suffering. Not that she believed him—she wasn't that stupid. But she was desperate and willing to try anything, and he did seem optimistic. She would grasp at any glimmer of hope.

Simon had been a difficult child from birth, but it was only when he started school that she had realised just how difficult. She sensed that other mothers thought she was exaggerating when she told them what she had to put up with.

He could never have been described as a contented baby. He was impossible to satisfy when she was feeding him, no matter what she gave him, and he became fussier about his food the older he grew. He was a light sleeper, too, and would cry a lot, and even as an infant he was awkward, crying when she picked him up to comfort him, and stopping when she put him down.

Once he was able to walk her father nicknamed him the Tornado. He devastated everything and everybody around him, but because he was so young and because they thought that his unsappable energies would ultimately dissipate, she and her husband followed him around picking up the pieces, imagining that eventually he would slow down, or that the whirlwind would be channelled into productive schoolwork and result in high achievement. They were convinced that everything they were putting up with would be worthwhile, that they had a child of enormous energy and potential, a genius, and that all they had to do was wait until he started school. He needed school, they said, from an early age—he should have started when he was three, he was certainly ready for it.

But it soon became clear that this was not the case. Unable to keep his mind on his work or to sit at a desk for more than five seconds, Simon ran around the classroom causing chaos and confusion. He was not used to sitting still or doing anything for more than a few minutes, and had always simply gone from one thing to another as his mind took him. He expected others to follow him and to allow him to decide what he would do. He reacted angrily when the teacher told him to sit down; and swore at her when she led him to his seat.

This kind of behaviour persisted and a special assistant was appointed to provide personal support, but matters only became worse. Simon ran from her and hit out at her for no apparent reason. If she managed to keep him at his seat long enough to do some work, he would rip it up at the slightest mistake, and when reprimanded by the teacher he would hurtle out of the classroom in his frustration and anger. If other children spoke to him or looked at him in the wrong way he would throw something, shout at them or lash out. On one occasion when he did this and the assistant tried to intervene, he stormed out of the room and climbed onto the school roof. Liz had lost count of the number of times she had been called to the school, but she remembered this one. He stood looking down at her and the headmistress, waving his fists at her. 'Fucking bitch! You would come! Bitch woman! I'm not coming down for you!' But he did come down, after everyone had heard him shouting. She felt terrible—an absolute failure. It was as though he had climbed onto the roof just to humiliate her.

She reacted by defending him, blaming the school and the teachers and the other pupils for the way he behaved, openly to their faces. She had one huge slanging match with the headmistress who seemed to hold her accountable for everything, and from then things just went from bad to worse. Nobody could do anything with him. Nobody was interested.

However, when he began to attack other children, including a small girl of six, there was a firm response. All the other parents complained; insisting that he had to go. He was a danger to himself and to others.

It did not take long to exclude him. Liz remembered having to leave work to go and collect him—immediately. She also remembered having to lie to her boss about why she had to resign so quickly, but she knew it was going to be difficult to find another school that would take Simon, and that she herself would have to look after him. After two months another school was found and at first Simon seemed to respond to the extra help he received. The pre-planning of his entry to the school had been thorough and efficient, but the tell-tale signs were still there for Liz. She heard that he was beginning to refuse to do any work and that he had been rude to the teacher. She recognised the glances of other parents when she collected him from school. She knew by the books he brought home that things were far from being as they should. Pages were torn, his writing was more like a vicious scrawl, a protest. He showed no interest in allowing her to read his book to him.

It seemed to her that nobody could explain why he behaved as he did and nobody seemed to care. All she was aware of was that nobody wanted him. He was excluded and nobody knew what to do with him.

In a way she understood. She knew that nothing had ever changed. He had always been unpredictable, restless and impulsive. She had never really known where she was with him, never felt that they connected. It was only after he had thrown a tantrum that she had ever been able to sense a response, some degree of warmth. How she had once imagined that he would fit into school she did not know.

It was his incessant talking and interrupting that ground her down. The fact that he never seemed capable of sitting still and listening, or just quietly amusing himself, made her wonder whether there was any point, whether there would ever be some feedback for her which would make it all worthwhile. He just kept on going hour after hour, day after day, and she became part of it. Time after time he bounced off her, hurt her and then cast her aside. She could have put up with it if she had known that there was a reason, if someone could have told her why.

She saw ahead only a life of misery and isolation. With Simon she could be nothing but his keeper. She could not work, she could never make friends because of him. She hardly dared to leave the house.

She could accept this, simply walk away from it or think the unthinkable and get rid of him. Perhaps she should just hand him over to Social Services . . .

It was one month after the doctor had visited. Liz was standing looking at the mantelpiece, holding it with two outstretched arms. She threw her head back and laughed aloud with an uncontrollable sense of joy. She felt ten years younger.

She had just had the most perfect time with Simon. He was now in bed, asleep, and the nine o'clock news had not even begun. They had shared a wonderful day.

On waking he had eaten his breakfast and cleared the dishes without having to be asked. He had brushed his teeth, washed and then dressed. She particularly remembered how he had said, 'Come on, Mum, we'll be late for the bus!' as they prepared to go shopping. When she thought of this it made her weep for joy. She wiped her eyes. It had seemed that she would never hear him speak to her like that, in an innocent, childlike way.

They had caught the bus without difficulty, and she had followed him upstairs where he found a seat next to a window. On the way into town he had pointed things out to her and listened as she explained what various buildings were and how she and his father used to walk this route before they were married. From his questions he appeared to be genuinely interested in what she was saying; she had sensed that for the first time they were sharing something together. During the morning they had had coffee in a favourite restaurant of hers, one to which she had always wanted to take him but had never dared. He had sat opposite her and asked her if she wanted him to pass the sugar; he had held out the plate of cakes to her and insisted that she have first choice.

Later he had followed her round the supermarket, passing items to her as she requested them, and pushing the trolley closer whenever she drifted away to collect something which she had forgotten. When her neighbour, Mrs Thompson, approached, Simon had noticed her among the shoppers and politely pointed her out.

'Shall we ask her if she needs any help, Mum?' he had asked.

In the afternoon she had decided to take him to the park. Her heart had sunk when she saw a number of children playing on the swings. They always complicated matters. The perfect day was about to be spoilt. 'Why are all these children here?' she asked.

But to her delight Simon ran on ahead and joined them. He gently pushed a small girl who found it difficult to get started, and then jumped on to a swing of his own, shouting, 'Give me a start, someone!' A small boy had heard him and gone over to help. She heard the boy say, 'What's your name?' and saw Simon turn towards him and smile. 'Simon,' he said, 'what's yours?'

Sitting on a park bench nearby she had been joined by another mother. They had chatted about the number of holidays which teachers seem to have, the weather, the opening of the new supermarket on the outskirts of town and the price of almost anything you could think of. They did not talk about their children at all until it was time to go. All the while Simon had happily played with the others. 'See you again sometime,' the mother had said. 'Nice to meet you.'

She and Simon had eaten their evening meal together at the table and not in front of the television. She had put out the best crockery and even a small bowl of flowers in the centre.

'Could you pass the bread, please, Mum?' he had said, and when he had finished eating, 'Thank you very much, Mum. That was lovely.' She had felt warm and content as she cleared and washed the dishes. Those few simple words meant so much.

The remainder of the evening had been just as perfect. They had watched television and he had played with his toys for a while. When he was dressed in his pyjamas and had on his dressing-gown and slippers, she had given him a biscuit and a cup of hot chocolate. She thought that she would always like to remember him like this. He was clean, calm and content. Bathed in the soft light of the table lamp he was her baby again. She loved him and wanted him.

'Time for bed,' she had dared to whisper. But there was no problem. 'OK, Mum,' he had said. 'Can I use my new toothbrush tonight?'

And now it was only nine o'clock and he was sound asleep. She knew this because she had already checked him twice. She relaxed into the luxury of the sofa and watched the news, but she did not hear what the newscaster was saying. She was going over the day again, trying to convince herself that it had really happened, that she had had such a wonderfully normal time with her child.

Suddenly she saw that the time was ten-thirty. She stood up, stretching to her full height, and made her way upstairs. When she reached the bathroom she looked carefully in the long mirror. Holding her hair away from her face she thought that she really ought to do something with herself. Her figure was still pretty good and a new dress, perhaps, or a blouse and skirt might help. She longed to tell someone, but for the moment she was determined to keep it just to herself, perhaps because the day had been so perfect for her, or perhaps because she feared that she would wake the next morning to find that it had been just a wonderful dream. All she knew was that, for the first time since Simon had been born, she was happy, and she wanted to stay that way for as long as she could.

She stretched out under the duvet and smiled at the ceiling. She tried to read a book which she had started months ago. She surprised herself by daring to think of what she and Simon might do the next day—she even found herself planning the following weekend when she could perhaps take Simon to see her sister— and what would her husband Peter think when he returned from his present contract? Confused by a mixture of excitement and anxiety, she found it difficult to settle comfortably. She wanted so much to remember this day, for Simon to stay as he had been. But would it be possible? Could a child change so much in such a short time, and if he could, how long would the transformation last?

2   ADHD

It had not taken Dr Good long to realise that Liz Jones needed help. From the description of her son's behaviour it was clear that both Simon and his mother were extremely distressed. If no action were taken, one or both of them could come to serious harm.

He called in to see Maggie before he left, and explained what he was going to do. If she could help by looking after Simon and by calling in to see Liz, he was sure that he could soon have things back to normal. He only needed time—about a month—to arrange things, and he was sure that after that Liz would be quite capable of managing. In fact, with a few days' rest she would most likely be able to have Simon back for short periods of time.

He was delighted when Maggie agreed to help, and reassured her that there was a good chance of Simon's behaviour being transformed. He had seen other equally severe cases of children with difficult behaviour, and met parents just as anxious and exhausted as Mrs Jones.

Although he did not mention it to Maggie, he thought that there was a strong possibility that Simon was suffering from Attention Deficit Hyperactivity Disorder.

SYMPTOMS OF ADHD

Pre-school signs

Distraught mothers describe their children as having been restless from infancy onwards, and many claim that even before they were born their difficult children moved around in the womb much more than their other children had done. As toddlers they never seem to stop and are continually on the move. When they start to talk they chatter incessantly and are into everything, going from one thing to another, exploring, climbing, hardly ever resting. In short, they are exhausting children. Both parents, despite their love for their child, breathe a sigh of relief when he or she finally drops off to sleep, but they cannot relax completely: they know that the child will not sleep for long and that once he is awake there will be another anxious day ahead.

Many parents, however, willingly tolerate this in the belief that their child is extremely bright. They do more than cope with the continually demanding behaviour, going to great lengths to provide more stimulation for their child, to expand her horizons further, to maximise her potential. Others, however, describe their difficult child as slow, lethargic and always day-dreaming. As a toddler, they say, he would play quietly—indeed, he appeared so content that they would sometimes forget he was there. He was a 'good' baby and was never any trouble. They are not worried when he does not respond to their efforts to stimulate him. They see their child as placid, one whose contentment indicates a wholesome degree of self-sufficiency.

Early schooldays
Most mothers do not realise that there might be a problem until their child starts nursery school, for coping with other children seems to intensify the behaviour traits of these difficult children. Those who have been hyperactive since birth clash with their peers. Because of their continual demands on others they are disliked and rejected. Their peers cannot tolerate their persistent high level of activity, their inability to settle to task; they find it impossible to form a friendship with a child to whom nothing seems important for more than a few seconds, and who is only ever concerned with satisfying his or her own impulsive needs.

Those who are described as slow and lethargic are at the opposite end of the spectrum. They are neglected, rather than rejected, by their peers. They make demands on no one and no one pays any attention to them. They appear anxious and attract no friendships.

Attention deficit disorders
Both types of children, those who are hyperactive and those who are not, clearly have something in common—an inability to focus, to stay on task—and this hinders their capacity to develop relationships. Attending school serves not only to highlight these problems but to make them worse. Because they have attention deficits they

find it difficult to do the work and because they cannot do the work or relate to others their behaviour deteriorates.

The hyperactive child, unable to sit still for more than a few seconds, will be made fully aware of this. In her frustration she wanders around the class even more and reacts angrily when reprimanded. Rejected by other children, she asserts herself in whatever way she can, refusing to do her work or even destroying it. She throws rulers and pencils about, shouts out at inappropriate times and does all she can to distract other children by interfering with materials and equipment, banging objects about and making offensive remarks. She will ultimately attack other children and assault the staff either verbally or physically. She stands a high risk of being excluded from school.

Such secondary symptoms are typical of the child with *Attention Deficit Hyperactivity Disorder*.

When faced with the shame of not being able to do his work and the taunts of other children, the child who is not hyperactive retreats into his own protective world. His self-esteem plummets and he becomes depressed and anxious, growing increasingly introspective and confused in an unfocused welter of self-examination and blame. There is a possibility that he may mutilate himself in an attempt to crystallise a sense of being, or that he may contemplate easing his suffering by committing suicide. He will have problems in school, but to a large extent these will go unnoticed. He is no trouble to anyone, but is regarded as a child with learning difficulties. If he comes to anyone's attention it is likely to be because his teacher feels that she is unable to give him the amount of time he so obviously needs.

Such a child can be said to have *Undifferentiated Attention Deficit Disorder*.

In our story it was clear to Dr Good that Simon had many of the symptoms of a child who had attention deficits and who was also hyperactive—one who might be suffering from Attention Deficit Hyperactivity Disorder.

DIAGNOSIS

Professional procedures

Once the diagnosis has been made there are clear procedures to be followed. The mother is referred to a paediatrician who interviews her to acquire more information. This specialist needs to know the full medical background of the child, including details of his birth and general development. He needs to know of any accidents or illnesses which may be the cause of the child's behaviour, and whether the child is taking medication for any other condition, and he also asks for details of the medical history of the whole family. He will want to discuss the child's behaviour to establish whether there are any clear patterns in the home and whether the mother is innocently helping to maintain these.

He also needs to ask the child's teachers about his behaviour and level of achievement in school, and in particular to describe how he relates to his peers. He consults with them in order to evaluate the child's strengths and weaknesses in relation to the programmes he will be expected to undertake, and he needs to estimate how far the school might be maintaining the child's behaviour.

Then the paediatrician will interview the child himself to observe him at first hand. To acquire all the information he needs he will administer a number of tests designed by experts specifically to assess whether a child has ADHD.

In order to do all of this he will begin by contacting the school's Special Educational Needs Co-ordinator, who will arrange the necessary meetings and generally see that an effective programme of treatment is quickly formulated and acted upon.

In Simon's case Dr Good was optimistic. He had seen what could be achieved, how suffering which had lasted for years could be relieved considerably by the accurate analysis of the condition and the implementation of an effective management programme. He felt that it would not be long before Liz Jones was smiling, but he knew of the dangers of making a hasty, uninformed decision. Once a child was labelled it was usually for life, at least in the child's mind, and one had to be as sure as possible of the diagnosis if one was to justify this.

*   *   *

You are probably desperate to acquire the kind of help which Liz Jones received, but you would be well advised to pause for a moment and consider my last point.

Providing a label for your child's behaviour is not going to be easy, and at this stage you should perhaps ask yourself whether searching for one is meaningful to you and worthwhile. I am sure that you think it is, but if you intend to ask your doctor to consider the behaviour of your child and to classify it with a view to treatment, you may find that you have inadvertently entered a minefield of conflicting views and opinions. Not all doctors are as optimistic as Dr Good, or so keen to make a specific diagnosis.

It will obviously be to your advantage if you have considered a few of the main issues which you might encounter.

Labelling your child

Many people would say that it is impossible to give a precise label to a child's behaviour because it is so complex, diffuse and unpredictable. Much of it is related to the setting and circumstances in which he may find himself. Also every child is born with a unique personality and will react differently to any given set of conditions.

Many parents and professionals do not like the idea of placing a label on a child. If a child is labelled 'hyperactive' or is told that he has 'Attention Deficit Disorder', they feel that there is a distinct possibility that he may live up to the definition by assuming the very image that they would prefer him to avoid. They fear also that the child might use the label as an excuse for his behaviour, and be encouraged to deny responsibility for his own actions. Difficult children have a strong tendency to do this anyway.

For these reasons the idea of labelling children repels many adults, but perhaps central to their thinking is a deep-seated fear of stigmatising their child, formally declaring that he is different from others. This is a common reaction which needs to be overcome and we shall discuss how to do this later in the book.

However, I imagine that at present much of your anxiety stems from the fact that you have never been able to get to the root of your child's problems, and that you would most definitely welcome a label for his behaviour. This may be because you feel that if you can find a label which describes his condition there will be a chance of discovering a cure, and if a cure is not available, an accurate diagnosis of his condition should make it clearer to you what can be done to help him.

In addition, you may find comfort from other adults who have formed support groups, and, rather regrettably, you may already have realised that it is only when your child has an officially accepted label that you stand any chance of receiving special help for him. Organisations which provide mutual support and present the case on behalf of those children who have ADHD are listed in Appendix A.

Professionals and the ADHD label

You should be aware that experts differ in their acknowledgement of the label ADHD. Some view its symptoms as a cluster of behaviours which should not be regarded as a syndrome and given a specific label. At the other end of the spectrum are those who see the symptoms forming a central syndrome which may have other conditions associated with it. In addition, professionals debate whether ADHD is predominantly a medical condition, or a condition which is determined by psycho-social influences.

Most of us would never consider bad behaviour as a medical problem. This may be because we have a natural wish to determine our behaviour, to be in charge of our own destiny. We are more than physical beings—we have free will and can choose how to behave. We look upon ourselves as being able to alter our attitude from within, or being able to alter our external circumstances. Thus we understandably resist the notion of administering medication to a difficult child who, according to our normal terms of reference, is not ill. We much prefer to say that her behaviour is a symptom of the way she is reacting to circumstances. If we adjust her environment or help her to cope with it the problem will disappear. This could be described as the psycho-social approach.

In contrast, the medical approach stresses that a child may

present difficult behaviour because of her physical makeup. If her difficult behaviour is persistent and pervasive to the point where it seriously impairs her development and the lives of those around her, then she should be provided with medical treatment. This may involve the administration of drugs and, as with the treatment of other conditions, the implementation of recommendations regarding the adjustment of her environment.

Most people would agree that when a child is ill his or her behaviour is likely to deteriorate or change. This is very often the first sign of an illness. They would, however, find it difficult, even with behaviour which is persistent and pervasive, to accept that it is a symptom of a 'permanent' physical condition.

You may not. Professionals and parents such as yourself who have to live or work with a very difficult child know intuitively that from a very early age there is something different about his behaviour. You have been able to feel the subtle difference when he was very young; when he began to mix with others it became glaringly obvious. But the inclination of most parents is to avoid thinking that there might be something wrong with their child—that his behaviour might be a symptom of a medical condition. They prefer to believe that his behaviour is a psychological phase or a result of the circumstances in which he finds himself—the situation is temporary and can be changed. The permanency of a physical disorder is too much for them to bear.

Labels and cultures

In the United Kingdom there is a strong preference for the psychosocial approach to ADHD. Although attitudes are beginning to change, British experts are still cautious about the whole matter. Some still question whether ADHD can be regarded as a syndrome, and the contrast between their approach and that taken by their American and Australian counterparts is reflected in the huge differential in the rate of diagnosis. For example, while American clinics reported that 22 to 40 per cent of children referred could be diagnosed as hyperactive, an English teaching hospital recently assigned the description to only 1.5 per cent of the received referrals. Although the different criteria used for assessment could account for this, there is definitely less enthusiasm in Britain for regarding ADHD as a medical condition.

Your child may already have been examined from non-medical perspectives by many experts: teachers, psychologists, social workers and even psychiatrists. If you live in Britain, it is possible that even if a psychiatrist has advised you that the behaviour of your child could be caused by the condition Attention Deficit Hyperactivity Disorder, he may still have resisted prescribing medication. On the other hand, if you live in the United States, you will know that 3 to 5 per cent of school age children are receiving treatment for the condition and that they are benefiting from a multi-modal approach, part of which will involve taking drugs. In Britain there is such rivalry between the medical and non-medical approaches to ADHD that the condition has been described by those in the psycho-social camp as a Trojan Horse, an invention whereby the medical approach can surreptitiously regain its ascendancy in the field of Special Needs!

Perhaps the contrasting approaches in Britain and the United States are a reflection of the two cultures: British people are sensitive to the moral and ethical issues surrounding labelling; the Americans are simply pragmatic—if a label can help, use it; if medicine works, prescribe it.

You may feel that none of this concerns you, but I hope that you are now aware that when it comes to the difficult behaviour of children there are vested interests, both academic and commercial, asserting themselves in what can only be regarded as a growth industry. When you are considering changing your child's behaviour you will inevitably encounter a number of these conflicting viewpoints.

But do not despair! While experts may still debate the nature of the syndrome, there is a growing consensus of opinion on the best way to control the symptoms: following the diagnosis of the condition, a multi-modal approach can provide you with almost instant relief. Your child's behaviour will change, and your joy will come from realising that this is possible. We shall discuss later the important matter of how you can achieve and sustain this transformation.

INDICATORS

For the moment you may simply want some indication of whether your child could have ADHD, whether there is a label to describe his behaviour. We have already mentioned some of the symptoms which indicated to Dr Good that Simon possibly had this condition; the following, however, is a more detailed description of Attention Deficit Hyperactivity Disorder to help you gauge the degree to which your child may be affected. Score one point for every question to which you can answer 'yes'. Read each description before you answer.

Attention Deficit Hyperactivity Disorder (ADHD)

ADHD is a psychiatric diagnosis that is applied to children (and adults) who are experiencing significant social and cognitive difficulties in important areas of their lives. There are three main aspects:

A   Attention deficit
B   Impulsivity
C   Hyperactivity

Note that:
1   these symptoms must have been present before your child was seven years old;
2   they should have been present for at least six months;
3   they occur more frequently than in others who have the same mental age.

A   Attention Deficit

This refers to the inability of your child to concentrate, to stay on task, to be focused.

CHECK

1   Is your child easily distracted?   _____

DESCRIPTION

The freer the situation the more difficult your child
    becomes, but even when the situation could be

described as being controlled for normal children, he is still easily distracted.

Whether he is supposed to be working or whether he is supposed to be playing, he will be paying more attention to what is happening around him rather than to what he himself is doing. He will flit from one source of irritation to another.

He is much better when he is on his own, but even then he will seem quickly to lose interest in what he is doing (see 2 below).

2   Does he find it difficult to sustain his attention?   _____

DESCRIPTION

He will not stay on task for very long, even when he is on his own.

When he is doing something which you know he enjoys, he will only do it for a short while.

You really are not too sure, though, what he does like doing—nothing seems to last. Watching TV is momentary; listening to stories lasts marginally longer. Even playing football is a transitory activity.

3   Does he go from one incomplete activity to another?   _____

DESCRIPTION

If you are able to start him on anything he is unable to finish it. He goes from one thing to another, never completing anything.

You cannot rely on him for a completed piece of work or a finished job. Even if he is playing a game he invariably fails to complete it. Give him the task of washing up and you will find it only half done.

4   Does he have difficulty in following instructions?   _____

DESCRIPTION

Even when you tell him clearly how to do something, he will be unable to carry out your instructions.

He will find it difficult to take messages, or to run errands for you.

He may have problems remembering telephone numbers.

5   Does it seem that sometimes he does not listen?   _____

DESCRIPTION

He will not be able to hear all that you say. His mind will be on other things, changing from moment to moment. He may hear part of what you say, but invariably much of what you say will not register.

6   Does he often lose things?   _____

DESCRIPTION

He will never be able to find things. He will leave his books and pens somewhere and be unable to remember where.

He will leave his clothes where he feels like dropping them.

He will appear to be incapable of looking after things.

He will be disorganised in all that he does.

B   Impulsivity

This refers to the inability of your child to control his impulses, to inhibit his behaviour.

7   Does he simply blurt out things when he feels like it?   _____

DESCRIPTION

He will generally be unaware of the consequences of what he says.

He will say something and if he bothers to think at all, do so afterwards.

He generally lets his heart rule his mouth.

8   Does he find it impossible to take his turn?   _____

DESCRIPTION

He will barge his way to where he wants to be,
  disregarding others.

If he wants something he will need to have it there
  and then. He cannot wait.

He finds it impossible to queue in an orderly fashion.

9   Does he find it difficult to play quietly?   _____

DESCRIPTION

He allows his feelings to have full rein when he is
  playing. He is loud and uninhibited.

It seems that he cannot hold himself together, that
  he needs someone controlling him 100 per cent
  of the time.

10   Is he always interrupting and intruding?   _____

DESCRIPTION

You can never finish a sentence without him interrupting.

He intrudes into your space when you are trying to
  do something.

He pushes and pulls you when you are trying to have
  a conversation with someone.

11   Does he play/live dangerously, unaware of the
      consequences?   _____

DESCRIPTION

He is a danger to himself and to others.

He has no thought for injuries he might sustain, no
  fear of the pain he might inflict on himself or
  others.

His play is erratic, boisterous and volatile.

C   *Hyperactivity*
12   Is he restless and fidgeting all the time?   _____

DESCRIPTION

He is hard to satisfy. He is not content for very long
     with anything you give him.

You always sense that he is unsettled and feel unable
     to relax in his presence.

Some children are able to while the time away and
     amuse themselves but he cannot. He always
     makes demands on you.

He annoys you by continually fidgeting. He picks
     things up and puts them down again for no reason;
     he taps his fingers on the table or kicks the wall
     as he speaks to you. He makes funny noises and
     pulls faces.

He never appears content or at rest.

13   Does he find it impossible to sit still or stay
      in the same place?   _____

DESCRIPTION

When he is at home he tends to wander around the
     house.

He is unable to sit at the table for long when you
     are eating.

He is unable to sit and watch television for long.

When he is shopping with you he tends to wander
     away; he will invariably go in the direction oppo-
     site to yourself.

When he is in school he will wander around the
     classroom at will and be unaware of the inappro-
     priateness of this.

Compared to his peers you would describe him as a
     human tornado: he will always be on the go, never
     in the same place for more than a couple of
     minutes.

14   Does he talk incessantly?   _____

DESCRIPTION

He continually chatters, moving from one topic to
     the next in no logical order. Even when he is

watching TV he will talk. He talks as he plays. CHECK
He is a non-stop running commentary on all that
comes into his mind.

TOTAL: _____

Scoring
When assessing the degree of ADHD your child may have you
must consider two factors:
a   The score you have registered.
b   The degree to which your child's academic or social performance is affected.
There are three levels of severity:

1   Mild:
    Your child would have scored eight or slightly above.
    His schoolwork and interactions with others would show little
    impairment.

2   Moderate:
    Your child would have scored around ten.
    His schoolwork and interactions with others would show some
    signs of impairment but these would not be significant.

3   Severe:
    Your child would have scored around twelve or above.
    His schoolwork and interactions with others would have
    suffered significantly because of the pervasiveness of his
    behaviour.

CAUTIONARY NOTES

You may now have some idea of whether your child has ADHD.
However, as we stated earlier, you should be very cautious about
assuming that this is definitely the case. There are many other
aspects of his behaviour to consider, some of which may never
have occurred to you. For example, when did you last have the
time or the inclination to look at yourself and your own needs? It
is extremely important to do this, not just for yourself but also for
your child, and I shall be discussing the matter more fully in
Chapter 6.

Associated conditions

You may not be aware that there are many other labels that could be applied to your child. His attention deficit, impulsivity and hyperactivity could be part of another syndrome. Attaching a label to difficult behaviour can become very confusing and is best left to the experts to decide precisely where the emphasis should be placed when it comes to treatment.

To help you appreciate the complexity of the task with which they are faced, let's look at some labels which have a close association with ADHD. By being aware of these you will be able to help the experts when they ask you for further information. Check your child's behaviour against the symptoms given below:

CHECK

1   Undifferentiated Attention Deficit Disorder (UADD)

A child with UADD has attention deficits but not hyperactivity. Such children account for 30 per cent of those with ADHD. A child with UADD tends to be:

underactive rather than overactive _____

slow to complete tasks _____

a daydreamer _____

lethargic _____

not impulsive _____

confused _____

on the periphery of groups _____

2   Oppositional Defiance Disorder (ODD)

Up to 60 per cent of children with ADHD will also display the symptoms associated with ODD. A child with ODD could generally be described as:

difficult _____

moody _____

irritable _____

defiant _____

negative _____

strong willed _____

stubborn _____

argumentative _____

3   Conduct Disorder (CD)

This kind of child has similar symptoms to the ODD
child, but also:

acts aggressively	_____
runs away	_____
steals	_____
truants	_____
destroys property	_____
tells lies	_____
sets fire to things	_____
inflicts physical cruelty	_____

4   Emotional and Behavioural Difficulties (EBD)

Emotional problems and associated behavioural
difficulties occur across the full spectrum of the child
population, including those who may be described
as having ADHD. A child with emotional problems
may:

have low self-esteem	_____
be very anxious	_____
be depressed	_____
find it difficult to relate to peers	_____
show apathy	_____
be irritable	_____
be withdrawn	_____
be sullen	_____
be aggressive	_____
swagger	_____
be excessively touchy	_____

5   Learning Disorders (LD)

A child with Learning Disorders shows a discrep-
ancy between potential (IQ) and actual achievement.
He or she will have difficulty in:

speaking	_____
reading	_____
writing	_____
spelling	_____
arithmetic	_____

Complex combinations

It is obvious that many of the symptoms of these conditions over-lap. A child who has emotional problems is likely to exhibit the symptoms of Conduct Disorder or Oppositional Defiance Disorder. A child who has learning difficulties will often have emotional problems which may reveal themselves as Conduct Disorders or Oppositional Defiance Disorders. You should accept this and not expect to distil the condition into one category.

The exercise may have led to the conclusion that your child has ADHD combined with one or more of the above associated conditions. This is the case with most diagnoses—so much so that ADHD is regarded by many as a syndrome that underpins practically all others. However, using specially designed tests, the experts will be able to provide you with more precise conclusions, laying the emphasis of the diagnosis more appropriately and so assigning a label to your child's condition.

But they would not only consider the labels I have already mentioned. They would begin by considering whether your child's attention deficit, impulsivity and hyperactivity were being caused by other medical conditions.

Other medical conditions

It is extremely important for any child who is presenting difficult behaviour first to be given a physical examination, for his or her inappropriate behaviour may be caused by a medical problem.

A child who finds it difficult to see or hear may appear to have an attention deficit, or to be impulsive; in her frustration she may become easily distracted and hyperactive. (The difficulty she has had in seeing and hearing may have gone undetected from a very early age.)

Another child may appear to have Attention Deficit Disorder, having moments when he switches off and stares into space. These temporary absences may, however, be indicative of a seizure disorder.

Hyperactivity may indicate an overactive thyroid gland, impulsivity could indicate a condition such as Tourette's syndrome,*

---

* A neurological disorder named after its discoverer, Gilles de la Tourette (1857–1904), characterised by tics, involuntary vocal utterances and compulsive swearing.

while anxiety and depression occur as illnesses in their own right and need to be recognised as such, as do other conditions such as speed and language deficits.

There are just some simple examples, but there are far more complex medical conditions which may be causing your child to behave in an excessively inappropriate way.

If you are seriously concerned about your child's behaviour, you should never presume that your first port of call is his teacher or a psychologist. You should always first take him to your doctor for a physical examination.

CONCLUSION

I hope that by now you have been able to estimate the possibility of your child having ADHD and have realised the complexities involved when it comes to making an accurate diagnosis of his behaviour. This process is clearly best left to those who have been specifically trained in this field and who have the experience and expertise to decide when it is appropriate to label a child and what that label should be. Once that has been determined, the appropriate treatment package can be designed.

The insight you have acquired into your child's behaviour by attempting this preliminary investigation may have proved useful from a personal point of view. You may for the first time have analysed what it is about his behaviour that makes him impossible to live with and you can use this information to good effect: we shall be discussing later the important part you play in the treatment programme.

So far the important message, illustrated by the story of Liz and Simon, is that you must not carry on regardless, to the point where you are a danger to your child and yourself. If your child is driving you to distraction with his hyperactive, impulsive behaviour, if he is causing severe difficulties for those around him both at home and at school, if he worries you because he is withdrawn and depressed and because he has no friends, then you must explain this to your doctor. You must not hesitate to seek help.

If, after reading these two chapters, you feel that he might have ADHD, you should mention this to the doctor. Treatment is available and your child may respond extremely well to it. However, you should not presume that he has the condition before a paediatrician has carefully examined all aspects of his case. Only a highly trained and experienced expert is in a position to arrive at that conclusion.

3   Causes of ADHD (and Cures?)

If you are the parent of a child with ADHD you may often ask yourself why she behaves as she does. You may blame her behaviour on the treatment she receives at school, either from other children or from her teachers. You may say that she is easily led, and that if only she could associate with the right group of peers her problems would be solved. Perhaps you feel that if you moved house, she would be able to get away from those who have been a bad influence on her. Do you sigh that if her school work were not so difficult, or if the teachers would take time to help her, everything would be all right? Do you believe that once her brother or sister leaves home things will improve; or that her poor behaviour would be transformed if only she wasn't 'wound up' by your partner? That if you could only afford to buy her the clothes she wants, or the computer that all her friends supposedly have, or take her on holiday, then she would be a pleasure to be with?

In all these ways you might blame other people for your child's behaviour, but in your deepest moments of distress, when the day has been absolutely horrendous, you may feel totally responsible for the predicament in which you find yourself. You have created this monster who now wreaks her revenge and destroys your life and the happiness of all those around you. Trapped in such a nightmare you are desperate for a solution.

If you are a teacher who is trying to understand the behaviour of a child with ADHD, you will most likely blame his parents for the problems he presents. You will assume that they are unable to control their child, or that they are too harsh with him. You may feel that they are inconsistent and that they present ambiguous and confusing messages, especially when it comes to what is right and what is wrong. They most probably argue a lot in his presence; there is undoubtedly a great deal of marital discord. You may even suspect that the parents abuse their child—psychologically if not physically.

If you are an enlightened teacher you might first ask yourself what *you* are doing that might be causing the child to present difficult behaviour. You might think about rearranging the classroom in such a way as to minimise problems with other children; you might examine the child's work to make sure that it is possible for him to do what you are asking. You might consider whether the child is behaving as he does because he is being bullied. You will have searched your heart and mind to find a solution, since your professional reputation depends on your ability to control classes and deal with disruption.

If nothing has worked for this child you will feel threatened every time he appears in your class. Before you even arrive at school you will have that gnawing feeling in your stomach which only ever occurs when you don't know what you are going to do, or when you know that you are likely to fail miserably when he confronts you. In such a nightmare situation you, too, will be desperate for a solution.

NATURAL CAUSES

I am sure that both parents and teachers who have employed many strategies with a very difficult child, all to no avail, will be eager to know how Dr Good achieved the dramatic change in Simon's behaviour, described in Chapter 1. Over the years Liz Jones and the teachers at his school had thought they were doing all they could to help Simon, but nothing had ever seemed to work. Then along came Dr Good and within a month Simon's behaviour had been transformed. Do miracles really happen?

When a child behaves badly it is necessary to look not simply at the world around the child but at the child himself. Most people forget this. Parents blame those who deal with their child, and among these, deep down, they include themselves. Teachers also blame the parents, and reflect privately on their own incompetence.

Dr Good first of all listened to what Simon had been like from a very early age: he focused on the child himself. Only later would he need to know much more about the way Simon had been brought up and how he was being managed, both at home and at school. He knew that when it came to dealing with difficult children it was very important to acknowledge that Nature had just as big a part to play as Nurture. He believed that he must first look at what he was starting with before he considered what he was going to do with it. This approach seemed to be the opposite of the way most parents and professionals worked, but he had found it to be effective. When he was looking for the reason for a child behaving badly he would examine first of all the hand that Nature had dealt the child.

When you consider the child at the centre of your concern you should do likewise. Whether you are a parent or a teacher, you should not begin by blaming others or yourself when your child misbehaves; you should first take a close look at the child. He was born with his own characteristics which react in a unique way to life's circumstances, and you must understand what these characteristics are before you can begin to help him. You must accept that Nature may be just as responsible as anyone else for his behaviour, if not more. Dr Good adopted his approach because he knew from his colleague, the paediatrician, that there was good evidence to support the theory that ADHD indicates a dysfunction in the chemistry of the brain.

Brain dysfunction
Research into chemical activities is proving to be the most promising of many attempts to understand the complexities of the brain. From what has been discovered, it would seem that children with ADHD have a malfunction with their neurotransmitters, the chemicals by which a message is sent between nerve cells, exciting the receiving cell and helping it to propel the message further. Such chemicals as dopamine, norepinephrine and serotonin regulate the way we think, the way we feel and, among other things, our capacity to pay attention. If they fail to do their job, as they appear to in ADHD children, then behaviour can be badly affected.

As ADHD is caused by faulty neurochemical transmitters it seems reasonable to assume that if any form of treatment is to be successful it must take this into consideration. Modern technology has shown that drug treatment can help these transmitters work more effectively, and in the process transform a child's behaviour.

For most people who try to find a solution to their child's

difficult behaviour this is the missing part of the equation, the piece of the jigsaw which they have never discovered, or which they have been unable to accept. It is only a small part of the equation—there are two other very important parts—but it was one which Liz Jones was willing to consider. It transformed her son's behaviour and gave her hope for the future.

Genetics

ADHD is an inherited condition. Many children have fathers who also had the condition when they were children; a smaller number have mothers who in their childhood may have been described as having ADHD.

If you have a child who has ADHD you may often see in him a reflection of yourself as you were when you were young. However, you should not feel responsible for his behaviour because of this. Your child is quite unique. He has many facets to his personality, and it may be that in your guilt you are being too selective in the emphasis you place on certain of his characteristics.

If you strongly suspect that you had ADHD when you were younger, and if you cannot avoid feeling guilty about producing a child who behaves in such an abominable way, you should draw consolation from the fact that he will most likely learn to live with his condition, just as you have. More than this: you can alleviate his problems almost immediately if you are willing to consider slotting the final piece of the jigsaw into place.

As ADHD has its origins in the genes, you must accept that you are not going to cure your child of his condition: you are going to help him to cope with it. I shall discuss the role that you can play in achieving this in Part Two. Medication can help you, and later in this chapter we shall look at drug treatment in more detail; in Chapter 4 we shall examine the reservations you may have regarding the alteration of your child's behaviour with drugs.

To begin with, however, let's consider some other popular ideas about what causes ADHD. You should study these carefully since there are elements of truth in each of them.

Brain damage

When children are extremely badly behaved many parents and professionals suspect that they are brain damaged. Their child's behaviour has been consistently so bad since he was born that they assume there must be something structurally wrong with him.

Parents might think back to complications during the pregnancy or during the birth of their child. In their desperate search for a reason for his behaviour they may attribute it to trauma which he may have suffered while still in the womb, to his premature birth or to an infection he had during his very early years. They may think back to the time when their child dropped out of his high chair or when, in his first attempts to walk, he fell and gave his head a severe knock. They may feel that his poor behaviour originates from that incident, that it is a result of his brain being damaged.

A child can become hyperactive or unable to sustain his attention because of brain damage, but not all children who have ADHD are brain damaged. It is clear therefore that it cannot be said that damage to the brain is the cause of ADHD. Equally, while some experts see a link between ADHD and complications during pregnancy or childbirth, the view is not supported by large-scale studies. You should not therefore assume that because your child's behaviour is seemingly unalterable his brain is structurally deficient.

This may confuse you. You may feel that if you cannot alter his behaviour, no matter what you do, then there must be something organically wrong with him. You would be right in saying this, but not in the sense that his brain is damaged. As I have mentioned when discussing brain dysfunction, it may be that your child's brain is simply not working as well as it should.

Food allergies

The notion that a child's behaviour can be affected by what he eats seems reasonable. Whatever we eat should affect the chemicals in our body and possibly the way we behave. Although experts who specialise in immune systems are reluctant to accept that this process can be applied to behaviour, many parents believe whole-heartedly in the food allergy theory and are convinced that changing their child's diet does alter his behaviour.

So popular is the concept that whenever hyperactivity in particular is mentioned it is now automatically assumed that it is caused by artificial colourings, preservatives and salicyclates. If a child is hyperactive these items should be eliminated from his diet. Other dietary approaches entail including rather than excluding items in a child's food intake, the notion being that unwelcome behaviour, rather than being an allergic reaction to food, is rooted in a chemical deficiency. Large doses of vitamins are recommended to alleviate the situation.

Perhaps dietary approaches are so popular because they provide parents with something tangible to do; perhaps they achieve a measure of success because parents are so keen for them to work.

Maybe their success, which is usually seen in the initial stages, stems from the fact that parents who take them seriously spend a great deal of time in the selection and preparation of food, and in doing this give clear, practical signals to their child that they care for him. They stop him eating certain foods and allow him to eat others: they exert controls and project parental responsibility. This makes them feel good and makes their child feel safe. The diet provides a point for mutual conversation and concern, and because of his increased sense of security the child's behaviour begins to change.

Perhaps it is the nurturing involved rather than the nature of the dietary approach which provides it with a measure of success, but whatever the reasons you may feel that the treatment is worth trying since so many parents vouch for it.

There are, however, some negative aspects to consider. Following your initial enthusiasm, the demands of implementing a strict dietary regime may mean that it becomes counterproductive. Both you and your child may begin to react negatively to the stresses it places on your relationship. The diet may also affect the way in which your child interacts with other children. For example, if he feels terrible, an oddball, because he is the only one who is never allowed a soft drink, you may be compounding his problem.

To avoid this you will need to explain fully to him why he should consider going on the diet, and allow him to make a personal commitment. You will need not just his agreement but his positive enthusiasm for the idea. Anything less and the diet will develop into an effective weapon for him to use against you. Also, a child with ADHD can be very manipulative, and you should be aware that he may use a special dietary need to shed responsibility for his poor behaviour.

The key to success is good preparation and a sensible degree of flexibility. You must also have a realistic approach and keep things in perspective. Experts who study children's behaviour know that there are no simple reasons or solutions, so keep an open mind and do not fall into the trap of believing that to control your child's behaviour you only need to monitor his diet.

Studies seem to show that while there are substances such as caffeine (tea, coffee and soft drinks) which can affect the level of activity in children, the reactions to foods vary with individuals. If you are keen to see whether your child is allergic to certain foods you could monitor the times when his behaviour deteriorates and note what he has eaten. More especially you could observe any particular cravings he has and see whether these are related to a change in his behaviour. If you feel that certain foods cause difficulties for him, exclude these from his diet and note any changes.

It may be difficult for you yourself to arrive at any conclusion; if you continue to feel strongly that you need to eliminate allergy to food as a cause of his behaviour you should consult your doctor. Under his supervision a comprehensive exclusion diet might provide the reassurance you need. You should, however, bear in mind that while the behaviour of a small number of children might be affected by what they eat, there is no conclusive scientific evidence that ADHD is an allergic reaction to food.

Lead poisoning

It seems reasonable to assume that noxious fumes of any sort will be harmful if they are inhaled: we are all conscious of the health problems created by modern city living. The general health of children who play in streets polluted with fumes from car exhausts is clearly at risk, and there is some association between hyperactivity, an inability to concentrate and increased lead levels in the blood. It may be, however, that a hyperactive child who rushes about more than others will inhale more. His hyperactivity may optimise the possibility of a degree of lead poisoning from car emissions rather than the toxic fumes causing his hyperactive behaviour. There may also be a link between ADHD and road accidents since highly active and impulsive children are likely to be more at risk than others.

Lead poisoning can occur in children and may result in brain damage, but it is rare. It cannot be said that it causes ADHD, since the majority of children with the condition do not have elevated blood lead levels. In relation to other forms of pollution, however, it is acknowledged that mothers who smoke or abuse themselves with alcohol are more likely to have children who suffer from ADHD.

Other medical factors
A child may exhibit the symptoms of ADHD if he has one of a number of other medical conditions (see Chapter 2). If he is receiving medication for epilepsy or asthma he may behave as a child who has ADHD, but his behaviour will be a side effect of the medication and will only be temporary.

THE MEDICAL TREATMENT OF ADHD

There is of course a whole host of environmental factors which can affect a child's behaviour and we shall examine these in Part Two as we discuss what parents and professionals can do to help the child with ADHD. The way you manage your child at home and the kind of programme which his school provides for him are the other two parts of the equation needed if you are successfully to transform his behaviour.

If nothing which you or his teachers have tried so far seems to have worked, then it may be that you should carefully consider allowing your child to receive medical treatment. More than 70 per cent of ADHD children respond well to medication. It enables them to become more focused, less impulsive and less hyperactive. They respond more appropriately and both parents and teachers feel that their commitment is worthwhile. In cases of persistent distractibility, impulsiveness and hyperactivity this aspect of treatment should be neither feared not ignored—indeed, it can very often be the cornerstone of success.

You would probably like to know what drugs may be recommended as part of a comprehensive approach to your child's problems.

Methylphenidate (Ritalin)

The most commonly used medication for the treatment of ADHD is the stimulant methylphenidate. The drug has been used since the 1950s when it became commercially available as Ritalin. The controversy that resulted from the administration of drugs to children promoted a great deal of research into its safety, following which experts concluded that the drug was safe and that it was beneficial to some children.

Giving a stimulant to a child who is hyperactive seems to make no sense, but it is thought that the drug works in that it promotes the efficiency of the chemical neurotransmitters which we discussed when looking at brain dysfunction. When it is given to a child he is better able to focus, becomes less impulsive and his hyperactivity decreases.

There is no evidence to support the notion that a child might become addicted to the drug; children do not experience a 'high' with these stimulants. They receive small dosages and if they have matters explained properly to them they regard the drug as a medicine. Nor does research suggest that they later become addicted to alcohol or other substances; in fact their attitude seems to be one of resistance to drugs, because of the inconvenience and associated stigma.

While some stimulants such as pemoline (Cylert) take four to six weeks to reach maximum effect, the effects of Ritalin can be seen in thirty to ninety minutes. It is taken orally and lasts for between three and five hours. It can improve a child's cognitive ability and studies have shown that it can enhance short-term academic performance by up to 40 per cent. Children who take Ritalin assume a greater degree of self-control. They become less aggressive and confrontational and more focused on their work. While these changes can be observed more easily in formal class-room situations, children on Ritalin are able to relate in a less antagonistic way to their peers when they are socialising or at play. The drug also works for children with Undifferentiated Attention Deficit Disorder (see Chapter 2), though not so dramatically as it does for those with ADHD.

It works not only with younger children but also with adolescents, although administering it to teenagers may be very much more difficult. They will do all they can to avoid an implication that there is something wrong with them; they want to be different from others but not to be regarded as deficient in any way.

Because those children who do take the medication become more amenable to others, parents and teachers have a more positive attitude towards them. Their new pattern of behaviour may in this way be reinforced by a novel feeling of acceptance.

Side effects

Stimulants have been used with hyperactive children for over fifty years. They are regarded as safe and non-addictive for those with ADHD, and side effects (which exist with all drugs) are minimal. If they do assume significance then the treatment is simply curtailed. Initially a child receiving stimulant medication may experience a loss of appetite or difficulty in sleeping. He may feel nauseous, have headaches, or become irritable or constipated, but most of these symptoms soon disappear as he adjusts to the drug.

There is no evidence that the drugs restrict growth. Long-term studies have eliminated this theory and consequently the need felt by some parents to give their child a drug-free holiday in order that he might catch up with his growth.

A small number of children may experience tics and in severe cases this may develop into Tourette's syndrome; some may experience a rebound effect whereby, a few hours after their last dose, they suffer withdrawal from the drug and their behaviour becomes worse than it was before they took the medication. Before treatment starts your child's doctor will want to know whether there is a history of tics or anxiety in the family, since if this is the case it would be unwise to administer stimulant medication.

Severe side effects to properly administered stimulants, however, are rare. Besides, whenever it becomes obvious that the benefits from taking the drug are outweighed by the inconveniences, parents simply inform the doctor. It is generally acknowledged that, compared to other forms of psychoactive medication, stimulants are safer and have fewer side effects.

If Ritalin works it can have a dramatic effect on your child's behaviour. If it does not, your doctor may simply recommend that he stops taking it and advise you that other forms of medication should be considered.

Tricyclic antidepressants
Impramine (Tofranil), desiprimine (Noraprimine) and amytripty-
line (Elavil) have been used since the 1970s for those children
who do not respond to Ritalin or who have experienced unacceptable side effects from stimulant medication. They are also used
for those children who in addition to UADD show signs of low
self-esteem and depression. In 70 per cent of those children who
receive the medication there are reduced levels of aggression and
hyperactivity and increased levels of concentration, but the medication requires a number of days to take effect.

Common side effects include constipation, a dry mouth, elevated blood pressure and confusion, and there are rare instances
of manic behaviour and seizures. Because of these rare but potentially dangerous side effects, those children who take antidepressants must be monitored very carefully.

Clonidine (Catapress)
Whereas Ritalin may be recommended for children who are mildly
to moderately hyperactive, Catapress is administered to severely
overactive and aggressive ADHD children, and often to those who
have the chronic disorder Tourette's syndrome. It is normally
recommended after stimulants and antidepressants have been tried
and have failed. Sometimes it is used in conjunction with Ritalin
for severe cases of hyperactivity, but it is not recommended for the
treatment of Undifferentiated Attention Deficit Disorder. It is sometimes administered orally but can be given via a skin patch and in
this form can maintain a constant blood level for up to five days.

It is usually two weeks before Catapress works and it may not
reach optimum effect for two to three months. Sleep patterns and
appetite usually improve and it can promote growth. However, it
has an inconvenient sedative side effect which occurs one hour
after it has been administered and which lasts between thirty and
sixty minutes.

NATURAL VARIATION

If you cannot accept that your child's behaviour is caused by a
medical condition, you may be happier with a psychogenic theory
which in fact is not that dissimilar.

Many experts believe that in all respects human beings find themselves on a bell-shaped distribution curve. We all know that in relation to our fellow human beings we have an intelligence quotient (IQ)—some people are very intelligent, others not so intelligent, and most of us are somewhere in the middle. Likewise in our physical makeup some are weak, others strong and the rest in between. In emotional terms, too, we exist on a distribution curve which goes from resilience to vulnerability: we have an emotional quotient. While most of us are somewhere in the middle, there are people at one end of the curve who are born with resilient personalities and at the other there are those who are extremely vulnerable. Children with ADHD could be said to have fragile, vulnerable personalities.

If you applied the theory of natural variation to the medical approach you might say that your child with ADHD is skewed towards that end of the distribution curve where neurotransmitters are inefficient. At the other end of the curve are those who can focus extremely well, make considered judgements and keep themselves under full control. The rest of us exist in between and have a range of abilities.

Both the medical approach and the psychogenic theory emphasise that there is variation in human beings at birth. It is not only our life circumstances which determine how we react: we are born with a varying range of assets in terms of attention deficits, impulsivity and hyperactivity.

The two approaches differ when it comes to treatment, but only as you might expect. The medical approach would involve administering medication to alleviate the problem with the neurotransmitters; the psychogenic approach would use a variety of techniques to improve self-esteem and personal congruence. Each approach would aim to strengthen a child, to optimise his efficiency and improve his quality of life.

CONCLUSION

Although experts debate whether ADHD should be regarded as a syndrome, the majority would accept that the behavioural characteristics of most children who exhibit the symptoms can be changed by medication.

ADHD would appear to originate in the chemistry of the brain which, although structurally sound, may be faulty in the way it transmits messages. In a large number of cases Ritalin can remedy this—precisely how is not known, although research into neuro-chemical transmitters is leading to a more accurate understanding. The fact that it can transform the behaviour of some ADHD children very quickly and without significant side effects is seemingly indisputable.

A non-medical approach to ADHD is to interpret the child's behaviour as symptomatic of an innate fragility. This may provide a more acceptable explanation, but when it is adopted at the expense of denying any consideration of medication it can prove very costly in terms of suffering for both the parents and the child. The aim of both the medical approach and the psychogenic approach is to help a child reach his full potential: the chance of doing this is vastly increased if the approaches are combined.

When you are faced with a child who presents difficult be-haviour it will be your natural inclination to alter things around him first to see whether this can bring about change. But if his distractibility, impulsiveness and hyperactivity seem resistant to all your efforts, then you should consult your doctor. Do not wait until you are exhausted and at your wits' end. If you do you are liable to damage yourself beyond repair and will be putting your child at risk. You will certainly not be in a position to help him. You should not be apprehensive at the thought of the doctor placing your child on medication. He will only suggest this if he feels that it is the very best course of treatment which he can recommend. He will not regard it as such if he senses that you lack enthusiasm, for he will be relying on your commitment for its success.

For many years Ritalin has been used as a treatment for children who have ADHD. It is safe and non-addictive, and if the treatment is stopped there are no withdrawal symptoms. It can be used where it is needed, either at home or at school or, to achieve maximum efficiency, as part of a comprehensive treatment programme involving the adjustment of routines and procedures both in the home and at school.

There is no known cure for ADHD, but medication can alleviate your child's condition and in the process bring you enormous relief. Combined with a psychogenic approach it can help parents, professionals and the child concerned to avoid years of unnecessary suffering.

4 Should I Alter the Behaviour of my Child with Drugs?

Whilst parents and professionals may be desperate to change the behaviour of some children, they are reluctant to use medication. They will try anything else and persist with it. Although their efforts may fail they are prepared to suffer enormous misery for years rather than accept that their child's behaviour might be rooted in a medical disorder.

Should you already know something about ADHD you will realise that there are two main issues surrounding the condition: firstly, people question whether it exists and, secondly, they debate whether it is right to use drugs to alter the behaviour of children. I hope that from previous chapters you have been persuaded to the view of researchers who claim that the condition does exist, that it has its origins in a dysfunction of the neurochemistry of the brain and that it can be successfully treated with stimulant medications. In this chapter I shall try to answer some of those issues regarding medication which may still cause you to feel uneasy. For convenience I shall use Ritalin as the example throughout, and I shall address parents rather than professionals although the latter will acknowledge that they too share these concerns.

FEELING UNEASY ABOUT IT ALL

Moral and ethical reasons

'It's wrong to alter behaviour with drugs . . .' If you feel that it is morally or ethically wrong to change your child's behaviour with drugs I would agree with you, but the idea behind giving your child Ritalin is not to change her behaviour but to alleviate a condition which is causing her distress. No matter how much you might sometimes wish that it were possible, she would never be given such a dosage that she would undergo a personality change.

The purpose in giving your child a drug would be to help her respond to the setting which both you and her teacher are going to provide (see Part Two). The drug is a small but vital part of treatment for some children: it is only prescribed when it is felt that without it a child is unable to respond to other forms of treatment. To administer medication that would in any way destroy a child's capacity for freedom of thought, or which might stifle her creativity and individuality, would be wrong. To change anyone's behaviour permanently with medication would be immoral and unethical since you would effectively be destroying her.

Administering Ritalin to a child with ADHD is no different from giving medication to a child with epilepsy. You will be helping her to control her condition and fulfil her potential. If this is your intention then you should not feel uneasy on moral or ethical grounds. But do be sure about how you feel about your child (see Chapter 6). Children sense intent from a very early age and if you are to persuade your child to take medication for her behaviour (see Explaining, p. 64), you will need to be clear about your reasons for doing so.

Psychological reasons
1   'She may use the label ADHD to excuse her behaviour . . .' I have already briefly mentioned this (Chapter 2), and because it is such a common and well-founded fear I feel that it is worth further discussion.

A child who has ADHD is constantly exhorted to 'smarten up', to 'be good', to be 'a nice girl'. The implication is that she is dumb, bad and unpleasant to be with. In this way she is condemned, and in her attempt to become accepted she may blame everyone and everything around her for her behaviour. Any personal responsibility will be shed at the first opportunity.

When such a child is told that she has the condition ADHD and that this is the reason for her behaviour, she may be considerably relieved but will often use the label as an excuse. The label may even promote the behaviour which warrants it: if the symptoms of ADHD become firmly embedded in her mind she will assume them as part of her identity. If she were to be told that the condition was biological and that it could not be cured, she might cast caution to the wind and become much worse that she was.

Many small children who are 'treated' for their difficult behaviour are abused in the process. They are spoken to by professionals who fail to appreciate that children do not have the maturity of an adult, or that to involve them in adult introspection can be extremely harmful. Accordingly, when asked to describe herself, a seven-year-old may earnestly say, 'I have a problem: I am hyperactive. I must not take soft drinks otherwise I will just go up the wall!'

You should not allow your fears in this respect to stop you considering whether your child has ADHD and whether she would benefit from Ritalin. To avoid these pitfalls and others simply requires a little forethought and planning (see Explaining, p. **000**).

2 'She may use it against me . . .' A child with ADHD or any other problem may use her medication as a weapon against anyone whom she feels is susceptible. Children with behavioural difficulties are usually vulnerable personalities and will use sophisticated strategies to defend or assert themselves.

Your child may threaten you by refusing to take her medication. To frighten you she may say that she hasn't taken it when really she has. She may say that the medication is making her feel unwell, when really it is not. She will only behave this way when she knows it will be to good effect. There is a fair chance that it will: if your child has ADHD it is likely that you will have become embroiled in her condition, and that when she makes such suggestions you will feed her with the reaction she wants.

You may think you are caring for her, but in this way you could be reinforcing her condition. I shall be discussing this in Chapter 6, but it is important for you to realise that it 'takes two to tangle', and that you should make a special effort to cultivate an attitude of separateness in the relationship you have with your difficult child. You need to be detached and in a position of control for her. She will not be in a position to use the medication against you if you explain matters to her (see Explaining, p. 64), and if you are aware of how she might try to control you with her drug.

3 'She may become dependent on it . . .' Your child may become psychologically dependent on Ritalin. She may worry when she

realises that she has missed her tablet and because of this begin behaving badly. This will only happen if you have failed properly to explain the treatment to her (see Explaining, p. 64) or if you yourself have not fully understood matters.

Your doctor or paediatrician will tell you everything you need to know about administering Ritalin, but one particular advantage of the drug is that it is not catastrophic if a dosage is missed. There is no need for anyone to panic. It is of course better if a dosage is not missed since the idea is that a constant amount will help your child towards a more consistently acceptable level of behaviour. In other words, the likelihood of her letting herself down, of having a psychological setback, will be minimised.

When you are thinking about dependency, consider how you yourself might become dependent on your child's medication. You should never make it into an essential crutch for your personal survival. If you are psychologically dependent on her medication there is a very good chance that she will be too, and that your relationship will centre around it.

Social reasons
'I don't like the idea of my child having a psychiatric condition . . .' If you say this you are putting yourself before the needs of your child. Maybe you are prejudiced against psychiatry because you feel that society attaches shame to mental problems: you are ashamed of having a child who may be described as having a dysfunction of the brain. The implication that you too may be dysfunctional, since the condition is inherited, is too painful for you to contemplate.

Clearly you should not have any prejudices, especially when there is a chance that by ridding yourself of them you might be in a position to stop the endless battle you seem to have had with your child since she was born. Besides, you might be surprised (or not!) that many adults, far from preferring to blame their child's behaviour on the way they have raised her, are relieved at the thought that her distractibility, impulsivity and hyperactivity are rooted in a medical condition.

Giving your child's behaviour a label may have many drawbacks, but when it is a medical label it may accord her, and you, a certain degree of social acceptance. People may be more willing to understand her behaviour if they know that there is a medical reason for it, and more likely to accept you if they are aware that you are providing her with the best form of treatment. Perhaps you would prefer to think of ADHD as a medical condition rather than a psychiatric one. The distinction is not important, but it may be useful to remind yourself that medicines are used to treat both the body and the mind.

Practical reasons

The urgency of diagnosis and treatment
You may want to believe that your child's behaviour will improve with age, that she will mature out of it, but the fact is that ADHD does not go away. In a sense it may to some extent, in that a child who has ADHD may gradually learn how to cope with it. To a degree she may adjust her lifestyle so that she can survive with her personal traits, just as we all do.

However, this process of adjustment is not easy for the child with ADHD. Because of her experience of persistent criticism and rejection, her condition inevitably promotes secondary behavioural characteristics. These symptoms are self-reinforcing, in that poor behaviour brings further criticism and rejection. Before she has had the chance to recognise her personal characteristics and adjust to them, the child with ADHD has assumed the image of a girl with Conduct Disorder or Oppositional Defiance Disorder (see Chapter 2).

This is why it is essential to recognise ADHD as soon as possible (see Screening, below). If a child is seen to have the condition at a pre-school age then special provision can be made for her when she begins to attend. Playgrounds and nursery schools can play an important role in this respect and should for this and other reasons be available for all children.

Screening
Some experts would recommend the screening of very young children in order to prevent the development of secondary behavioural characteristics. The earlier the age the more chance of success, for in essence the difficulties of children with ADHD are to be found in their interactions with others. The longer they

are at school, untreated, the worse their predicament becomes.

Screening does not simply mean labelling and giving out the pills! It involves identifying specific behavioural characteristics, avoiding labels of any sort as far as the children go, and designing appropriate educational programmes. Simple techniques, such as placing a child near the teacher's desk, may be employed if the child with the characteristics of ADHD has been observed prior to attending school. In this way major problems caused by a disruptive child may be avoided. Only when it was felt necessary would Ritalin be recommended, and this would usually be after many other such adjustments in both the home and the school had been made. Three to five per cent of children have ADHD, and although this may not seem a great many, it indicates at least one child in the average classroom. This child will be very disruptive unless special provision has been made (Chapter 9).

An inability to relate in a positive, meaningful way to others can lead to loss of self-esteem and further negative interactions. The process is self-reinforcing and spirals downwards. If undetected, ADHD can lead to failure not only in relationships, but in academic and practical work. It often culminates in drop-out or exclusion, drug abuse and delinquency. You should never therefore believe that the terrible problems experienced with a child will simply disappear as she gets older. The young child with ADHD needs help before she develops into someone who is beyond control.

You should therefore welcome a screening process. It may help you to eliminate a multitude of future problems for your child, either directly or indirectly.

EXPLAINING

At some stage a child with ADHD will need the condition explaining to her. Although a very young child may without explanation be placed on a treatment programme, as she grows older she will want to know why special arrangements have been made for her. If you are to avoid the negative aspects of your child being diagnosed as ADHD (see Psychological Reasons, p. 60) you will need to consider how you might approach matters.

Who does the explaining?

You are the only person who knows how you relate to your child and because of this only you can decide what your best strategy might be. Do not assume, however, that you are necessarily the best person to do the explaining. If you have already reached battle stations with your child, you should seriously consider whether it would be better for someone else to do it.

Children respond very differently to people outside their immediate family and often feel much more able to express their thoughts and feelings to them. Vulnerable children in particular find it difficult to relate to those close to them. Your child may be like this. Most children have a local hero, someone in the extended family or neighbourhood, whom they respect and admire. Perhaps you might consider whether it would be appropriate to ask such a person to explain matters to your child. Your doctor might be the best person, or there may be somebody you know, who is liked by your child and who himself suffers with the condition. This may be the ideal person to approach.

You may think it strange to suggest that your child talks to someone other than yourself, but if you feel that the relationship you have with her is negative, then it is important to look to those who can help you. By involving a neutral third party you could avoid the possibility of your child refusing treatment for her condition and consequently a further deterioration in your relationship. As discussed earlier, children on medication for any condition may use it to manipulate matters in their own interest, and those who receive it for behavioural problems have a powerful weapon at their disposal. Somehow you need to defuse it before you give it to them.

General principles

1 Use the theory of natural variation

A central part of an explanation should be the theory of natural variation. I have already mentioned this in Chapter 3, but it is important. We are all different and the notion that we should all be the same is wrong and counterproductive. Everyone has assets and liabilities, but because we are all different we are able to help those who are less fortunate; we all benefit in that our weaknesses are counteracted by the strengths of others.

You should carefully consider and absorb this principle. If you allow it to flow through your thinking you will be saying the right things to your child. You will be accepting her rather than rejecting her. You will be saying that she is unique, that she has a definite contribution to make and that you are there to help.

2   Promote self-control

A difficult child needs firm controls and boundaries for her behaviour (see Chapter 5), but when it comes to medication you must accept that only she will make the final decision. If your child senses that you are imposing treatment on her she will use it to control and manipulate you. If you promote the notion that she is in control of matters, that she can decide whether to accept the treatment or not, then you will be negating any tendency she may have to use the condition as an excuse for her behaviour.

You may feel that your child will respond to your firm guidance, and that it would be wrong to present her with choice, but do ask yourself whether you are overemphasising the importance of the matter. It is essential not to do this.

3   Minimise its importance

If you overemphasise the importance of treatment your child may become anxious, feel threatened and refuse to cooperate.

Bear in mind that although her behaviour may be of great concern to you, it is something which both you and she have lived with for years. You must be cautious in your approach. If you rush into things and overplay the issue you will only meet with resistance. By minimising its importance you will be denying her the opportunity to use it against you. If she senses that it is vital to you that she accepts treatment, she may refuse. If you explain matters to her appropriately (below) you will express care for her but not anxiety.

4   Be straightforward and honest

You must always he honest with children. The inclination of some parents is to tell their child that her medication (in the form of a pill) is to keep her healthy and strong—the whole family may pretend to take it. But the child will know that she is different from her peers, that she has some sort of problem which makes them dislike her. She will be aware that you are making excuses. At a very early age your child is able to detect your intentions and should you be anything but truthful with her you will find that sooner or later it will backfire on you.

Being honest does not mean being brutal and unfeeling in your approach. In fact, if you are going to be successful in persuading your child to undertake a long-term programme of treatment, you will need to think very carefully about how you might provide the right kind of positive motivation. A factor to consider in this respect is the age of your child.

5 To younger children

At all costs you should avoid introducing a young child to the world of labels. She may use the symbol ADHD as an excuse for her behaviour. You should also avoid introducing her to the world of symptoms: she will simply say that her behaviour is caused by her distractibility, hyperactivity and impulsivity—and carry on!

Your strategy should be to identify her enthusiasms and interests and explain matters in those terms. Do not labour explanations and keep them simple. Your child may be interested in computers or animals: take these interests and use your imagination. Here is an example of how you might begin to explain.

Child's interest: cartoons

DISTRACTIBILITY

Select a character such as Bambi and comment on how he stops and listens to hear the sounds in the forest. He concentrates hard and is able to hear the sound of a raindrop, even though birds are singing and the wind is making the trees of the forest sway.

Can your child do this, or does he find it difficult to pick out sounds? Can he hear what the teacher is saying in the classroom when others are talking and doing things?

Every child is different. Some children find this easy and some find it hard. If they find it hard, they may not hear the teacher when she is telling them something. They may hear the sound of other children talking and turn to see what is happening; they may see the goldfish swishing in the tank, but they do not know what she has said.

When she asks them a question they cannot answer because they have not heard what they were told.

On occasions even Bambi finds it difficult to concentrate, and when he does he becomes frightened because he knows it can lead to trouble. But he knows what to do if it ever happens.

Some time ago, when everything was going wrong for him, when he seemed to be forgetting everything and getting into a great deal of trouble, when his friends called him names and would not play with him, he ran into the forest and by chance discovered a beautiful princess. She listened to him and comforted him. When he left she gave him a small box. 'Take these,' she said. 'They may help you.'

Inside the box were small pills like this . . .

HYPERACTIVITY

You could select the Roadrunner and observe how he seems to zoom all over the place, never stopping for a moment.

What makes him do that? Why is he dashing about all the time? He never seems to sit still. What does your child think would happen to the Roadrunner if he went to school? Would he be in a lot of trouble?

Some children are like the Roadrunner and some are not. Those who seem to keep out of trouble are those who can sit at their desks and who do not have to keep moving around all the time.

Those pills that Bambi was given could also help the Road-runner . . .

IMPULSIVITY

If your child watches *Tom and Gerry* she will readily acknowledge that Tom is always in a lot of trouble because of the way he acts before he thinks. He always seems to do the first thing in his mind without stopping to work out what might happen, and he never learns. No matter what he does, Gerry makes him look like a fool. While Gerry does the thinking, Tom simply goes with his feelings.

If your child were one of these characters, which would she rather be? But is she really like Tom?

Some children are like Gerry, and some are like Tom. Most are somewhere in between the two: sometimes they stop and think and at other times they cannot control themselves. Those pills that Bambi had would have been useful to Tom. They would have helped him to stop and think, just as they could have helped the Roadrunner to stop moving around all the time . . .

This example illustrates how you might approach the matter with a younger child. Her school and home management programme can be quietly adjusted around her and in this way she might be gently motivated to accept medication.

6 To the older child

With an older child it will often be more appropriate for a third party to explain ADHD. In this case the relationship you have with your child is more likely to have deteriorated to the point where, no matter how you try to explain matters, he will react negatively.

You will be able to estimate how this may apply to your child, but most children who are untreated by the age of eight or nine will have serious secondary behavioural characteristics. They will already be highly manipulative because of deep-seated feelings of rejection and will be resistant to anything they are told by those who are close to them. You should therefore enlist the help of someone outside your child's immediate social circle (see p. 65).

Whoever explains ADHD to the older child should, as with the younger child, first attempt to establish his personal interests. These can then be used to great effect.

Personal heroes

Most people have personal heroes, ideal models whom they would wish to emulate. Children are no different, and between the ages of eight and twelve they begin to build informative mental images of real life personalities. These people become significant role models in their lives and can be used to introduce ADHD.

Unlike the kind of explanation which you might present to the younger child, you should not coat the message in metaphor or try to disguise it in any way. Their heroes are not characters from cartoons or fairy tales.

Interest: soccer

If your child is interested in soccer you could discuss this with
him. You could ask him who his favourite players are, who he
would like to be and why. You should encourage him to discuss
the qualities of players in detail. You should make the point that
they all have different skills to offer their team. Each has his part
to play.

DISTRACTIBILITY/IMPULSIVITY/HYPERACTIVITY

Some players seem to be very steady team members. Even under
great pressure they can be relied upon to remain calm. Because
they can do this they rarely make mistakes.

Others seem to have sudden urges to do things, and very often
add a flash of brilliance to the game. Without them the team would
often appear drab and uninteresting, but they do make mistakes
and get the team into all kinds of trouble. They don't seem to
think things out as much as others do. Sometimes they appear not
as members of the team but as individuals, doing their own thing.
Sometimes it works and is exciting, but most of the time they
look as though they are dashing about all over the place and to
no good effect.

Which of these kinds of players would your child prefer to be?

In this way you could lead the child into discussing his difficulties. You could then tell him about ADHD and how it can be
treated. When you do this, bear in mind that you are talking to a
prospective teenager and take note of the points raised in the
section below.

6   To teenagers

The way in which you would broach the subject with a teenager
is very different from your approach with a younger child! Children, and none more so than teenagers, will react with anger if:

a   they cannot get their own way;

b   they feel that they are being criticised;

c   they sense injustice.

Hopefully, if you are discussing matters at this stage, you will be
talking about some aspect of your child's treatment rather than
introducing her to the notion of taking medication. However, in
either case here are some suggestions:

(i) Always create a scenario in which your child is making the decisions. Never give the impression that you are imposing your desires or opinions on her. If she wants to have her own way and you want her to accept treatment, allow her to make the initial decision and you will have fewer problems.

(ii) Never project criticism. If you discuss matters with her, be careful not to imply that her behaviour is unacceptable. Her behaviour is as it is, and when she has made the decision that she wants to change it, she will accept treatment. Any further admonitions will wash over her.

(iii) Always explain matters in full detail. If you try to hoodwink her she will sense injustice and unfairness and will react negatively. Treat her as an adult. Simply give her the full facts— anything else will be interpreted as a lack of respect. She may respond as a mature adult if you explain the condition as described in Chapter 2 and in particular the theory of natural variation discussed in Chapter 3.

You may find it more appropriate for a professional to explain matters to your teenage child—without your being there. If she is given the opportunity on her own to speak to your doctor or paediatrician, she may feel able to express her concern and fear without losing face. If you are there you become the issue for her and she will be in no position to do other than reject anything that is said in your presence.

If it is difficult to arrange this for your child, you should make sure that you have books and pamphlets available for her which explain ADHD. Suitable reading material for both younger and older children can be acquired from the sources mentioned in Appendix A.

CONCLUSION

If you accept the view of experts that ADHD exists and that it has its origins in the neurochemistry of the brain, it would seem logical that you should accept their equally firm opinion that medication may help to alleviate the condition. Yet you may still be apprehensive about the whole approach and more particularly about giving your child a drug to control her behaviour. Perhaps you feel that there are too many psychological, social and practical sides to the problem, or maybe it is the difficulty of trying to explain ADHD to your child and the fear of the battles you are going to have with her over treatment.

I hope that in this chapter I have helped to clarify matters. Remember that Ritalin is not addictive, there are few side effects and if you are at all unhappy there would be no difficulty in taking her off the medication. Whether your child responds positively to the idea of receiving treatment for her behaviour will largely depend on who provides her with the initial motivation and how this is done.

If your child is presenting you with difficult behaviour which is both intense and persistent, you should never accept that you must both somehow live through it: one or both of you may fail to survive. Visit your doctor and tell him of your concern. You have everything to gain by providing him with an opportunity to analyse your child's behaviour. If your child does not have ADHD the doctor will, from the diagnostic process, be able to indicate to you what your child's specific difficulties are and to suggest ways in which you might help her.

The reason why you wanted to read this book was probably because you were seriously concerned about the behaviour of your child; it may have seemed to you that there was no hope for the future. Like Liz Jones you had tried everything and nothing had seemed to work. When you consider your apprehension regarding the use of medication to improve the behaviour of your child, compare it to the fear which you presently have for her future.

5 Other Reasons for Difficult Behaviour

Although I have stressed that ADHD is a biological condition, it is important for you to realise that when we are considering a child's behaviour we must take into account both his innate characteristics at birth and the way in which he is brought up. So far I have emphasised the biological aspect of behaviour since most parents and professionals are inclined to forget it. They presume that if the environment is right an unwanted behaviour will disappear. While this may be the case for most children, it is not the case with those who are diagnosed as ADHD. These children have a biological condition which requires medical treatment: for this to be fully sustainable and effective, special consideration must also be given to their home and school environment.

In this chapter I would like to make final preparations for action by considering some notions which may help you in the work you undertake with your difficult child. By taking these into account, you may be able to adjust your approach to make it more effective. My intention is not to encourage you to be self-critical in relation to what has happened in the past, but to help you to create a new approach to your child in the future.

Difficult children will often require you to respond on the spur of the moment, and if you are exhausted and at your wits' end (as you probably are for most of the day) you will need to be well prepared. Many children with ADHD have a capacity for unbounded originality when it comes to patterns of behaviour, and to cope with this you must be clear about your underlying stance.

If the beliefs you have about the needs of children are firmly crystallised in your mind, and if you have a small, manageable number of considered aims, purposes or beliefs, whatever you do at that moment of crisis, the time when you switch to automatic mode, has a good chance of being appropriate.

To help you establish these I have included some searching personal questions. If you answer them with complete honesty your approach will be considerably enhanced. It would be a good idea to share your thoughts with a friend. He or she will keep things in perspective for you, and by sharing your thoughts and feelings you will inevitably be stronger for your child.

These are very important exercises. Do not rush through the questions. Have a paper and pencil ready, choose a quiet place (your local library?) and look upon this as an opportunity for you to have some special time.

Although I address parents, teachers are urged to imagine themselves as the parent of a child with ADHD, and to give the questions serious consideration. Only by projecting themselves into this position will they be able to come close to experiencing the pressures under which parents operate on a daily basis. A good idea for them would be to choose a child from their group who has ADHD symptoms and to imagine that they are his parent (I hope this would not be too traumatic an experience!).

A child's difficult behaviour is often the result of his needs not being met. We shall look at these needs from the point of view of the child, the home and the school.

THE PSYCHOLOGICAL NEEDS OF CHILDREN

1   The need to have a clear picture of the world

A child needs to feel that he has certain people in his life who will always be there. Certain events must always occur; certain rules must always apply. He must know where he stands in relation to everything around him. He needs a map of his personal world, one which can be recognised and where the compass points do not change.

QUESTIONS

Whom do you think your child would regard as the significant
   people in his life?
What do you think they represent to him?

Choose three events which your child would regard as regular
markers in:
a each week;
b each month;
c each year.
List three golden rules which are unwritten but always assumed
by your family.

2 The need to have an objective in life
A child needs to have a level of expectation to which he can work.
He needs to know that there are certain rules that are beyond him,
that cannot be questioned. He needs to sense that there are certain
objectives for him to achieve. These objectives need to be in the
interests of others, not just himself.

QUESTIONS
Do you exhort your child to achieve, or are you happy to let him
create his own standards?
Would you say that your style of parenting is an accepting one or
an expecting one?
Do you involve him in all decision-making, or do you believe that
there are some things which are the domain of parents and
others which are the domain of children?
Can you remember the last time you did something for another
person or for the community, and did you share this with your
child?

3 The need to feel part of things
A child needs to feel a sense of relatedness. He needs to be able
to see himself as part of a whole. He needs to sense that he is of
value to others, that he is part of a network of relationships, a
network that gives him a sense of identity. He needs to belong.

QUESTIONS
Make a list of those who form your child's social network (those
mentioned should have a significant relationship with him):
six friends;
four relations outside of your immediate family;
two adults who are not related to him.

Write down the last time:
  a   you and your child visited someone in his or her own home;
  b   your family gathered together with your child present;
  c   someone visited your home with your child present.

4   The need for stimulation

A child needs stimulation (see p. 164). This will help to develop his language and his capacity for abstract thought. It will also help to develop his inner controls. Severe boredom can lead to severe problems: children have been known to mutilate themselves or even kill others in an attempt to feel a sense of their existence.

QUESTIONS

When was the last time you switched off the television and did something different with your child?

What are you particularly interested in, and do you think he senses this?

Computer games may be attractive to all children, but do you worry that your child might soon be brain dead from staring at his monitor for so long?

What have you done to encourage your child to be active rather than passive?

5   The need for a sense of rootedness

A child needs to bond with his mother. This happens in the very early stages of childhood and provides an anchor point for future development. With this foundation he can become a separate person with a sense of independence, free will and self-control. If the bonding does not take place with his mother or another significant person, he may later attempt to form a similar relationship with others and either try to control them (sadism) or be controlled by them (masochism). He may become excessively fond of himself or have a craving to destroy.

QUESTIONS

Do you feel that you connect with your child?

Does he seem to connect with others?

Is he cold with you or excessively clingy?

Does he become anxious when you leave him?

Do you feel happy with the warmth of his relationship with you, or does it cause you concern?

6 The need for love

The sense of love, of unconditional acceptance, is built into the bonding process with a child's mother; we also believe, however, that it can be achieved in a slightly different form with others. Unconditional acceptance is not the only component. It is just as important to recognise that love means caring, and that caring means trying to provide all the needs which we have already mentioned.

QUESTIONS

When you admonish your child do you sometimes feel that you genuinely hate him?

Do you think he is aware of your hatred?

Is your love for him conditional on his behaviour?

If the doctor told you that your child was suffering from a condition that caused him to behave as he did, would this make you hate him any less?

A SUMMARY QUESTION

Do you think that your family offers your child:
1   consistency?
2   a sense of purpose?
3   a sense of belonging?
4   stimulation?
5   a sense of attachment?

If you have been honest you will have found it painful to answer some of these questions, but by giving them consideration you will be clearer about your aims when you are dealing with your difficult child. Most parents find it difficult to provide precise answers, but if you found them particularly searching it may be an indication that your child does not have ADHD. Perhaps his behaviour is simply a reaction to his life circumstances rather than symptomatic of a biological condition. This should not depress you: it should cheer you. In Part Two I shall be discussing the many things you can do to effect change.

On the other hand, you may have had no difficulty at all in recognising the points I have been making: you may have been fully aware of all these needs and you may have tried extremely hard to meet them. If this is the case there is a good possibility that your difficult child has ADHD and that the only ingredient missing in your treatment package is the medication. However, at this stage the matter of diagnosis is not our concern. We have covered this and the medical approach to ADHD in previous chapters.

The purpose of asking questions that relate to your child's needs was to help you appreciate some of the psychological reasons which may be at the root of his difficult behaviour, and to look at how you may help him in the future.

Feeling threatened

We all use certain techniques to defend ourselves when we feel threatened, and because of their condition, children with ADHD are more defensive than most. The consequences of their distractibility and impulsivity have made them less sure of themselves and more sensitive to criticism. They do not have to throw chairs about and shout to signal their vulnerability. Other, more sophisticated techniques are employed. We all use these, but children with ADHD or emotional problems need to employ them more often.

Defensive reactions are used to protect our self-image; if we were to lose this we would become insane. If we have a strong image of ourselves, if we know who we are and what part we play in a clearly defined world, then we can resist attack. If, however, we are unsure of ourselves, if our self-image is weak, then we will interpret many interactions as a threat.

Broadly speaking, there are three techniques which we use to defend ourselves:

1 We counterattack with verbal aggression or sarcasm.
2 We distort information to suit our purpose.
3 We avoid what we do not want to hear.

A child with ADHD may avoid situations which pose a threat. He may refuse to go to school (see below) or to the Cub Scouts; he may not express himself for fear of destroying the world as he knows it. He may avoid issues in the most obvious way by withdrawing into his own world of apathy or fantasy or he may act in a way which is seemingly totally bizarre and unrelated to any threat that you may perceive. In this way he will be displacing his feelings. When your child is causing you severe problems, you should interpret his behaviour as a sign that he feels threatened. If you do this you may find that your reaction to him becomes more positive.

This is easier said than done, since a defensive child will often appear to be anything but vulnerable. But you should recognise loudness and swaggering as a sign of inner weakness, just as much as you would quietness and withdrawal. If you realise this you will appreciate that to counterattack would be inappropriate since you would only make his condition worse. Try to answer the following questions:

1 Which defence mechanism does your child use the most?
2 List three situations in which you could guarantee a defensive reaction from him.
3 Why do you think he feels threatened by these situations?
4 How do you react to his defensive mechanisms?
5 When you feel threatened, what technique do you use?

FAMILY MATTERS

Changes, relationships, and circumstances

The questions you answered above addressed some deep issues which may underlie your child's behaviour. However, the causes of his behaviour may be much simpler, in which case you may assume that he does not have ADHD, or that if he does, these could be aggravating his condition. In either case you would benefit by giving them consideration: you can do no harm by eliminating possible sources of distress.

You will be aware from experience, and by learning of the needs of children, that they react adversely to change and stressful circumstances. The child with ADHD has a special need for consistency, and his behaviour has a greater tendency to reflect circumstances around him. When change suddenly occurs, when some significant person disappears from his life, or when there is a degree of uncertainty, he will become anxious. Sensing a lack of external control he will give full rein to his impulsivity and become more distractible.

The following questions may help you to eliminate possible sources of aggravation within the family:

CHANGES
1   Has a member of the family recently left home?
2   Has a new member arrived?
3   Has there been a bereavement in the family?
4   Has the family recently moved house?
5   Have there been any other significant changes?

RELATIONSHIPS
6   Have you and your spouse started to argue a lot?
7   When did your relationship with him or her change?
8   Have your other children been particularly difficult?
9   Do you feel that you have no time with your child?
10   Do you expect too much of him?

CIRCUMSTANCES
11   Have you had problems with the neighbours?
12   Have you had financial problems?
13   Have you had health problems?
14   Is the future uncertain in any way for you or your spouse?
15   Do you have relatives or someone to talk to?

Residential special education

Bearing in mind of your answers to the above questions, here is another, very difficult one: Is the family the best place for your child? This is an issue which most parents of a child with ADHD are driven to contemplate. Few, however, give it the serious consideration it deserves, since most people assume that the family is the safest place for a child. They believe that it provides him with a feeling of belonging; within a tightly knit group he will feel safe and secure and all his needs will be met.

Nonetheless, family groups can be violent, since it is within the privacy of the home that members can unleash their emotions, confident that they will suffer no loss of reputation or social standing; they can express themselves freely without necessarily losing friends or colleagues. Within the family members learn to live with the full range of human emotions and in this way it can act as a safety valve.

Whereas a resilient child may benefit from this, a vulnerable child will become frightened and more anxious. The child who has ADHD may suffer considerably from the frank interactions and verbal exchanges which can be expected in most homes. His state of distractibility may be aggravated by confusion or disturbance, and arguments or even slight disagreements may be difficult for him to manage; he may escalate problems with his excessive impulsivity and hyperactivity. Because he cannot make sense of what is happening around him, when he feels unsettled he may shout or throw a chair at someone. He will do the first thing that comes into his head and will add to everyone's problems by continually rushing around. He will easily become engaged in the family dynamics and in turn will embroil everyone in his personal predicament.

Although children who have ADHD need not be emotionally vulnerable, a large percentage of them are and many may find it difficult to cope with those who mean most to them—the family, and their mother in particular. Emotionally vulnerable children are disabled in terms of coping with their feelings and family dynamics could prove too much for them. Thus, while the family can be a place where personal growth takes place without risk, for the more vulnerable child it can be a setting where, in the absence of careful planning, personal frustrations are exaggerated and expressed.

When you are considering the needs of the child with ADHD you should therefore recognise the importance of making special arrangements in the home; you should not presume that it is up to the child to fit in, that the onus is on him to change his behaviour. If you feel that you have done all you can, and he is already being treated with medication and receiving special attention both at home and at school, you should face up to the question of whether the family is the best place for him to be. He may need to be away from the family and in a situation where he can receive the necessary degree of consistency and environmental support. He may need residential special education. Should all else fail, this can provide the best setting for the child with ADHD (see p. 178).

Family size

Children who come from large families differ from those who live in small ones. They have a lower level of verbal intelligence and reading attainment, possibly because there is less intensive interaction and less opportunity for the development of effective communication skills than there is in small families, and because less encouragement is given for academic attainment. They may suffer from overcrowding and material hardship—parental discord and conflict are often rooted here—and the level of parental control and quality of discipline may be jeopardised. Accordingly, children from large families are more restless, disobedient and destructive. They tend to bully and fight more than children who come from small families.

On the other hand, children from small families may suffer from overindulgence by the parent. An only child is often regarded as precious: he may have been born under difficult circumstances after a period of sterility, a series of miscarriages or deaths of other children. It could be said that he is overvalued and therefore overprotected. A parent will have excessive contact with him; she will mother him for too long, excluding all other relationships; she will prolong the process of infantile care, bathing and feeding him and generally being at his beck and call; she will prevent any move towards independence by not allowing him to help around the house, and by trying to fight his battles for him. In many instances she will be emotionally dependent on the child and, if she was raised in a home lacking warmth and love, may be determined to give her child all the love she herself missed. If she has no social life with her partner she may compensate by investing emotionally in the child, recognising the futility of her marital relationship.

The effect on the child is to increase his level of disturbance. The child with ADHD may display heightened levels of distractibility, hyperactivity and impulsivity should any of these factors assume significance.

The following questions are intended to help you examine your own situation. You may not be able to alter anything, but pondering on these issues may help you better to understand the behaviour of your child.

If you have a large family:
1 Did you have a favourite child?
2 Did you spend an equal amount of time with each child?
3 Think of each child and describe him or her with one word.
4 Is it your experience that children from small families generally do better academically?
5 Is it your experience that children from large families are generally more aggressive?

If you have a small family:
1 Do you think that if you had more children you would regard any of them as less precious?
2 Do you think that you are overprotective and too anxious about your child?
3 Have you a tendency to want to fight his battles for him?
4 Do you feel that you have a life of your own, without him?
5 What is the ideal number of children to have in a family?

Position in the family
The firstborn in a family is likely to be a higher achiever, both scholastically and at work, than those born later; the last born is prone to scholastic failure. The firstborn, however, is more likely to develop an emotional disorder. While he may receive more love and attention than his siblings, his parents are likely to be more anxious, pressurising and controlling than they are with their other children. The eldest child has also to adjust to the arrival of the others. Often there will be a regression in his toilet training on the birth of the new baby; the problem is usually transient but regression may persist in this and other ways, especially if the parent punishes the child for his behaviour. A hostile relationship often exists between siblings when there has been an intense and warm interaction between the parent and the first child; a rather more detached relationship between the parent and the firstborn will result in an amicable interaction between the two children.

The arrival of a second child always changes the dynamics within the family. Whether or not any of the members will be adversely affected depends on too many factors to enable one to be precise about the long-term effects on a child, but we must be aware of the central part that his intrinsic vulnerability may play.

If he is not very resilient within himself he may react extremely badly to the arrival of another child; if he himself is the new arrival he may be badly affected by the hostile reception he receives from his sibling.

Whether a child comes from a large family or a small one and whether he is the first or last child does not necessarily mean that he will present you with behavioural difficulties. The family is a phenomenon in which there is a great interplay of variables; the size of the family and the ordinal position of a child within it are just two of these. Each child will react differently to his family circumstances according to the strength of those around him and his own level of resilience.

When you are considering the behaviour of a child with ADHD you should take these matters into consideration. He has to live not only with a dysfunction in his neurotransmitters, but with the situation into which he was born.

Here is an exercise to help you clarify your thoughts: you will need a pencil and paper and the help of a friend who knows your family.

1   Without your friend seeing, write the names of your children on separate pieces of paper. Turn over each piece and write on it two words which would describe that child. One word should describe his or her academic ability; one should describe his or her temperament.
2   Show your friend the descriptions and ask him or her to name each child correctly.
3   Turn over the papers and see whether you agree.
4   Do you think the descriptions of the children would have been different if they had been born in a different order? Has their ordinal position been significant?
5   Discuss the position you held in your family and how this affected you and your siblings in practical terms:
     Did you go to bed at different times according to your age?
     Were clothes passed down?
     Who was the most articulate?
     Who was the most intelligent?
     Who got the most attention, and why?

6   Looking at your brothers and sisters now that they are adults, do you feel that the ordinal positions they held as children had any bearing on their present status? Who has been the most successful?

You may have concluded from this exercise that all children must be affected in some way by their ordinal position. It is important to bear this in mind when you are considering the behaviour of a child with ADHD. The stress experienced by all children in relation to these matters strengthens most and could be said to promote the rich variety of personalities we come across. But if a child has an innate problem with regard to his ability to concentrate and to control his impulses it can aggravate his condition. If he is the firstborn, he may experience severe and prolonged regression; with no control over his impulses he may attack his baby brother. If he is the new arrival he may be unable to cope with the hostile reception he receives from a sibling. In his uncertainty, and at the mercy of his impulses, he may feel confused and rejected.

Significant people
Children who present difficult behaviour often come from families where the lines of communication and authority are blurred. When members discuss matters they do so in a negative fashion and no clear decisions are ever reached. This may be because there is no one person in the family who is strong enough to take responsibility.

In normal families there is no fixed pattern of dominance which could be said to cause children to behave badly. Fathers make decisions and mothers make decisions, and some are made conjointly. Problems arise when conflicting messages are given by a parent—when, for example, a mother by her facial expression gives one message and by her voice another. Problems also arise, especially for the child with ADHD, when because of parental discord there is no firm agreement on anything. Children need to have a clear picture of family relationships; ambivalent feelings between parents will only add to their problems. Far better for the child if the warring parents were to separate.

Other complications for the child might be caused by grandparents who live too close to the family. While the parents of a problem child need to recruit the help of others, it is often a fatal mistake to involve close family members.

Grandparents in particular often seem to overinvolve themselves with their grandchild when he is in some way disabled. Their intentions are always honourable, but the effect of their intrusion can be disastrous. A child who is experiencing no difficulties is usually spoilt by his grandparents; the child who is vulnerable can be damaged beyond repair. Grandparents are removed from the realities of daily life when it comes to looking after a difficult child who may be manipulative, self-centred and quite capable of behaving nicely for the short time that his grandparents are available to spoil him.

Grandparents can transmit conflicting messages to the child; often the essence of the problem is that they tend to make decisions for the parents, and the child becomes confused over who is in charge. This happens to its worst effect when the grandparents are living almost on the family doorstep.

The grandparents are not the only participants in this scenario. We have them and the difficult, manipulative child acting their respective parts—and of course the parents, who have most likely relinquished control out of sheer exhaustion.

Every child, not least the child with ADHD, needs significant people in his life outside the home and the extended family. Such people as youth leaders can provide a safety valve not only for the child but for the family. The child may model himself on them and will more readily listen to them than to his parents, since because of their emotional distance they can give him clear and unequivocal signals.

QUESTIONS

1   Who makes the decisions in your home?
2   Do you present conflicting messages to your child?
3   What are the benefits of having an extended family—from your point of view?
4   Do you agree that there are drawbacks to having relatives who live too close to you?
5   For how long can you put up with your parents?
6   Do you feel that it would be counterproductive to have them around permanently?

SCHOOL MATTERS

A child may begin to present behaviour problems when he starts school. This could be an indication not that he has the condition ADHD, but that he is a vulnerable child who reacts sensitively to others. On the other hand he may have the condition, and because of attention deficits may feel threatened by the smallest demand the school makes on him. In any case, it is worth bearing in mind that all children experience initial difficulties of some kind when they begin school, and some suffer more than others. Should you have a child whose behaviour in the home clearly deteriorates, it may be that he is having problems at school.

Whether he has emotional problems or ADHD, he will develop the characteristics of a child with Conduct Disorder or Oppositional Defiance Disorder (see Chapter 2) if you fail to take the necessary action. To allay any concerns regarding your child's behaviour you should have no hesitation in making an appointment to have an informal chat with his class teacher. Only when parents and teachers act in partnership is it possible effectively to address the needs of children (see Chapter 10).

School work

Because of their distractibility and impulsivity many children with ADHD find schoolwork too difficult, and once they are left behind their behaviour deteriorates. Teachers who fail to recognise their symptoms may present such children with inappropriate work and then brand them as lazy or uncooperative.

Some children may be seriously concerned about impending examinations, and be unable to take the pressure exerted on them by the expectations of both teachers and parents. Children should be allowed to work from things they can do to things which they cannot, but often they are given work which at their age they should be able to do but which they find impossible. A child with ADHD suffers more than most in this respect because he often appears to be so very lively, quick and intelligent. The fact that he cannot easily concentrate and retain information is often overlooked.

Class size

A child with ADHD may be intelligent but have difficulty in absorbing and retaining information; he may find it more difficult than most to hear what the teacher is saying in a large and poorly controlled group setting. The amount of personal attention he needs will demand a good staffing ratio and effective classroom organisation (see Chapter 9). If the group setting is too large and staffing ratios are too high, a child at either end of the curve of natural variation (see Chapter 3) will suffer. Neither his specific learning needs nor his emotional needs will be met.

Other children

Children make heavy demands on each other and only gradually develop the social skills which allow them to sustain relationships. The child with ADHD finds it difficult to remain focused and this, combined with his impulsivity, means that he inevitably makes more enemies than friends. He may feel that he wants to join the group but because of his innate condition cannot: in his frustration he will begin to behave badly.

Special arrangements need to be made for the child with ADHD to alleviate potential problems. He may benefit from social skills training and appropriate grouping strategies (see Chapter 9).

Bullying

Bullying occurs in all schools, from nurseries to secondary schools, and all children are at risk. Good schools establish a clear anti-bullying policy, the aim of which is to create a safe environment for all children; even so, because of the secret nature of bullying, it is impossible completely to eradicate it. A child with ADHD is more at risk than others: because of his inability to make friends easily, he may begin to bully or, as a victim, withdraw into his shell (see Chapter 9).

Teachers

A child's behaviour may deteriorate when he feels that a teacher is picking on him. Invariably children are going to dislike certain teachers, and when a child is experiencing difficulty with his work he will often focus on the shortcomings of the teacher concerned.

A child with ADHD who is failing in his work, or whose

condition is aggravated by an inappropriate classroom setting, will quickly develop anti-social behaviour. He will become disruptive and, particularly in a large class, will be classified as a nuisance. Without the resources to manage his behaviour the teacher may deal with him in the only way open to her: she may threaten him or even bully him.

In Chapter 9 I shall be looking at what schools can do to help the child with ADHD, but for the moment here is a list of questions which may help you to focus your thoughts on the problems your child may face at school. Again I stress that it would be extremely beneficial if you were to discuss these outside your family, with a friend:

1 Think carefully, and try to remember how you felt on your first day at school.
2 Describe a teacher from your junior school. When you think of him or her, how do you feel?
3 What was the worst thing that ever happened to you at school?
4 Was there a subject which you dreaded? Why did you dread it?
5 Was there a child whom you disliked at school? Why did you dislike him or her?

CONCLUSION

I began Part One with a story, the purpose of which was to illustrate the daily suffering of the parent of a child with ADHD. I hoped that the story would strike a chord in the minds of other parents who are reading this book because, like Liz Jones, it is possible that they too have reached the end of the road.

Thinking she was sacrificing all for her son, Liz struggled for years—but only towards the verge of a nervous breakdown. She finally reached the stage where the stress of continually having to control her child drove her into a state of apathy. On the day the doctor was called she was totally exhausted and had lost the desire to get out of bed.

Yet within a short space of time the world had become a much more pleasant place for her. She felt happy and alive: her son was behaving and she had begun to see a future for them both.

It was not that Dr Good was a miracle worker, he was simply well trained. When he heard what she had to say about Simon he knew that there was a distinct possibility of a full and speedy recovery—for them both. He consulted his friend the paediatrician and between them they arranged a suitable treatment programme which involved themselves, the home and the school.

Part One has focused primarily on that piece of the jigsaw puzzle which most people forget, or prefer to ignore when they are dealing with the behaviour of a very difficult child—namely the biological basis for his behaviour and the need to treat it with medication. In the second part of this book we shall examine the two other components which are essential if the jigsaw is to be complete and the treatment is to be sustained and effective: the special adjustments which should be made in both home and school for the child with ADHD. However, we shall begin by considering the need for you to take a close look at yourself. Before you can deal with a difficult child it is important that you address any personal issues which may affect your relationship with him.

Part Two

HELPING THE CHILD WITH ADHD

6 How Can I Survive this Child's Behaviour?

Many adults interpret a child's behaviour from just one viewpoint: they invariably think of a difficult child only as the result of a poor upbringing. Her parents are regarded as inept and her teachers as incompetent. They assume that if parents did their job properly and teachers worked harder, then all children would behave well.

This attitude may be based on their assumption that when we are born, and especially with regard to our emotions, we are basically all the same, with an identical capacity to feel. Given similar settings we would all interpret the world around us and interact with it in the same way.

Such a way of thinking denies that we are born on a curve of natural variation but may be easier to accept because we feel that we are only able to change the environment: we can do nothing about the way we were born. It may also prevail because when most children behave badly, it only takes some minor adjustments to the home and school environment to effect change.

It is not an attitude which you, as parents and professionals who deal with children who have ADHD, can afford to adopt. If you were to think this way you would quickly be driven to desperation. As a parent you would feel that you were the cause of your child's behaviour and be ridden with guilt, and both you and your child's teacher would go insane making fruitless attempts to remedy the situation with constant adjustments to your child's environment. Regrettably, however, parents do invariably blame themselves for their child's behaviour, and professionals continue to support the popular notion that when they are faced with a disruptive pupil someone, somewhere is being negligent.

If you are to survive the behaviour of a child with ADHD you must first learn to focus on her (rather than anyone else) and to make a realistic assessment of her needs. I hope that in Part One

I have helped you to do this. If you are in any doubt about the best course of action, you should take her to a doctor. Remember that difficult behaviour can be caused by a medical condition; your child may have fallen and hit her head on something without your knowledge, or she may have an illness which is difficult to detect. She may have ADHD.

You should bear in mind that your doctor is there to help you not only with your child's physical ailments, but with her emotional problems and any associated learning difficulties: he will know where to refer you for specialist help. Do not struggle on year after year with your child, imagining that her behaviour can only be caused by something you are doing wrong.

If you want to make a fresh start with your child, you need to focus on yourself and to consider the way in which you think of her. This determines your relationship and could be adjusted to both your advantage and hers. Therefore, before considering the many practical ways in which you can help the child with ADHD in both the home and the classroom, we shall begin by taking a closer look at how you feel about her, and about yourself.

You and your child
When you are dealing with children it is important to realise that your attitude towards them may affect their behaviour. Nowhere is this more evident than with a child who has ADHD. Because of previous experience the child may regard you with apprehension, expecting to be criticised and rejected. If you approach her in an anxious frame of mine, she will most probably fulfil your expectations.

A child who has ADHD is likely to be more sensitive than others and will react adversely to any feeling of insecurity. If you think of her as a threat there is a good chance that you will provoke a defensive reaction from her; if you see and interpret her behaviour differently, you may find that it changes according to your attitude. A great deal of our apprehension of difficult children is caused by ignorance. We are not sure how we feel about them, or how we feel about ourselves when faced with one of their disruptive outbursts. We are not sure what it is that makes us feel as we do when we have been through one of these traumatic experiences.

In this chapter I shall ask you a number of questions to help you clarify how you feel about your difficult child. I hope that you will answer them seriously and afterwards read my comments. The questions may seem trite and of no value, but they are intended to help you think deeply about yourself, so take your time in answering them. The more deeply you think, the more you will be able to create an effective personal approach to the child with ADHD.

There is therefore no time limit to the questions and exercises. I would suggest, however, that if you are answering a question in less than five minutes you are missing a golden opportunity to get to know yourself just that little bit better. It is important for you to read all the questions and my comments, even though some are addressed to specific people. If you do this you may come to a greater appreciation of the way others see the difficult child. You will need a pencil and paper, and time when you can be away from your child. Please note that you are not allowed to use yes and no answers.

QUESTION ONE: TO PARENTS AND OTHERS

Do you see your child as:
1 self-centred?
2 a disappointment?
3 an embarrassment?
4 a nuisance?
5 frightening?

Comments
1 If you see your child as self-centred, I presume that she makes you feel unwanted and insignificant. She may not appear to take any interest in you; she may seem able to exist on her own. The world seems to revolve around her.

If she makes you feel like this it could be because you are not strong enough in yourself. When she is hyperactive, impulsive and seemingly concerned only with herself, in your weak state you become upset and confused. This may be because you need her more than you think, and resent it when she appears to disregard your presence.

The answer could be (1) to become independent of her and more of a person in your own right (we shall discuss how to approach this later in the chapter) and (2) to remind yourself that her behaviour is a reflection of her condition. If your child has ADHD she will, because of her distractibility and impulsivity, appear to be self-centred; combined with hyperactivity this may present her as a loud, egocentric and obnoxious individual. By regarding her behaviour as an indication of her medical condition, and by seeing yourself as a separate person, you may be able to think more objectively about things. You will be in a better position to provide for her needs.

2   If you see your child as a disappointment, it may be that from the very beginning you had false expectations of her. All parents have a mental picture of how they would like their child to grow up. There is also a tendency for them to relive their lives through their children. Some parents do this more than others.

If you have a fixed idea of what you would like your child to be, then you will either be disappointed or, if she conforms, she may be unfulfilled. Children should be regarded as individuals, emotionally attached but increasingly separate from their parents. Parents should recognise also that their children will continually change. If you have expectations which are beyond her capabilities, the behaviour of your child with ADHD will deteriorate: she will become more distractible, impulsive and hyperactive. She is more sensitive than others to failure and will express her frustration.

Her present behaviour may be a disappointment to you, but if you are to understand her you should ask whether her behaviour is a reaction to your unrealistic demands, or a reflection of your own sense of failure in life. If you are unhappy with your lot, there is a good chance that you will inflict your disappointment on her.

Imagine that instead of having behavioural problems your child had epilepsy. Would your attitude to her be any different? Remember that ADHD is a physical condition. Could you still say that she is a disappointment to you? To say this implies that she can control herself, but is choosing not to. If you maintain this stance you will make little progress with her for you will be starting from a position of rejection rather than acceptance.

3   If you see your child as an embarrassment it is clear that you see her as part of yourself. You should not do this. If you see any child, and especially a difficult child, as an extension of yourself you will become more and more frustrated. You must regard her as a separate, unique individual who is related to you through birth. You care for her and love her, but you are not responsible for her characteristics.

Again, you are not seeing her as a child who is disabled; you are still looking upon her as someone who has full control over her distractibility, impulsivity and hyperactivity. She is consciously and deliberately causing problems and you do not want to be associated with her. You should see your child's behaviour as a symptom of her condition. She has to learn how to cope with this and you must help her.

Perhaps she is an embarrassment to you because she seems to reflect all your worst points. If you feel this you should ask yourself how much of your personality you project onto her behaviour and why you do this. Do you think that perhaps you live too much under her skin, that you try too much to do her feeling for her? A solution may be to become strong in yourself, to assume your own identity, and to stop trying to live through your child.

You should explain her disability to your friends—you will have to do this if you are to succeed in helping her. If you take time to explain her difficulties to others, there should be no need for you to feel embarrassed. When explaining matters to them be careful not to do this in front of her, since you may promote the very image that you would hope to extinguish.

4   If you see your child as a nuisance and getting in the way of other things which you may wish to do, she will sense this and feel rejected. On the other hand, if you wish to see her behaviour improve, you yourself must have some strong personal interests other than her. This should not present a problem if you have hobbies and leisure interests and are genuinely enthusiastic about pursuing them; she will appreciate that you are not rejecting her but fulfilling one of your own needs. She will benefit in that she will have a more clearly defined picture of who you are and what you stand for; you will become a separate person in her eyes, not just an extension of herself.

If you have no personal interests, see this as something requiring immediate attention. Do not be afraid of your child's reaction when you first attend that nightclass, or when you first go jogging. Unless you become stronger in yourself you will never be able to help her. If you have recruited friends to help you (see Chapter 7), you will have explained this plan of action to them and they will realise that it is part of a definite strategy.

It is important for your child to realise that she is not at the centre of the universe. A difficult child will tend to think this, and her parent will usually accommodate her. If you really care for your child you will see it as your duty to do something separate from her. You need to see yourself as being something more than an exhausted and frustrated parent; she needs to see you as someone who has strength; she will sense this if she knows of your other interests in life. She will of course feel rejected when you first leave her, but if you are going with the interests of both of you in mind, then with time the strategy will work. If you see her as a nuisance you will neither leave her nor return to her in the right frame of mind; you will be faced with an escalation in her poor behaviour and will soon lose your helpers.

You may say that you will soon lose your helpers anyway because your child will relish the thought of you going out and will lead them a merry dance on your departure. This kind of thinking will get you nowhere. You are back at square one, with your life centring around your highly manipulative and demanding child. You must put yourself first before she can begin to receive your help.

It may be hard for you to do this, but to be kind you have to be realistic. You must again think of your child as being handicapped and look at the situation objectively. Prepare your helpers and take the risk. Ask yourself what will happen to your child if you do not.

5   If you see your child as frightening, then it is clear that you have lost control, over her and over yourself. You must begin by gaining control over yourself. Start with the following exercises. You will find it very useful to go through them with a close friend. A good way to do them is for each of you to complete them on your own and then to discuss them with each other. Sharing can make you stronger.

To do the exercises properly you will need to be in a quiet place, so use this as an opportunity to be away from your child.

EXERCISE ONE: THINKING ABOUT YOUR CHILD
Answer the following questions:

1 Can you remember where you were at the time of your child's birth, and how you felt when you first held her?
2 How much did she weigh? Did she have a lot of hair?
3 How did you choose her name?
4 Can you remember the first time you took her out to see a close relative?
5 Can you remember when she took her first step?

EXERCISE TWO: THINKING ABOUT YOU AND YOUR CHILD
Write down the dates and details of the three most critical points in your life, the three most important crossroads.

1 Crisis number one:
2 Crisis number two:
3 Crisis number three:

Take your time over these. Remember where you were and who you were with. Try to go back into these times. Remember how you felt. Where did your child fit into these events? Was she born before them or afterwards? Was she part of the scenario?

It is important for you to look at your life closely. You may not think that this is relevant to the matter in hand, but if you are feeling that your child is out of control you must accept that it could be you who are weak. You may have lost the strength to exert control over your child because, like Liz Jones (Chapter 1), you have lost faith in yourself.

I would like you to do a further exercise. It is simple but could take up to thirty minutes to complete. Do not rush. The more details you can include, the more effective the exercise will be.

EXERCISE THREE: THINKING ABOUT YOURSELF
Complete the following for yourself, not for your child:

Name:
Date of birth: Place of birth:

Weight at birth: Baptised at:
Mother's name: Father's name:
Brothers' names: Sisters' names:

1 Schools attended, with dates:
2 Names of favourite teachers:
3 The worst things that happened to me at school:
4 What my ambition was in junior school:
5 My first day at work:
6 My first boss:
7 The first holiday I paid for:
8 The worst thing I have ever done:
9 The funniest thing that ever happened to me:
10 Where I was, who I was living with and what I was doing at the age of:
   a eighteen years:
   b twenty-five years:
   c thirty-two years:
   d forty years:
   e forty-five years:
   f at the present:
11 My proudest achievement in life:
12 The most important people in my life, and why (at least three):

Having completed these exercises you should be aware that your past life can offer you a great deal of strength. Although you may feel that your life has been rather mundane, it has been unique and is far more complex than you would at first imagine. You have lived through a great deal—I hope that as you tried to complete the questions you discovered this. More importantly, I hope that in attempting the exercises you realised that you have a wealth of experience to draw upon—a source of strength.

The exercises may also have helped you to understand your child. You may have appreciated that the state of your affairs could have been too much for her to cope with; you may have discovered in looking at your past that you were not so different from her when you were a child. ADHD is inherited; it may be that you too have the condition but have learned over the years to live with it, as indeed most people do.

None of this should upset you: if you can look at your past and not be afraid of it, you will feel stronger and better able to cope with your child. You will understand her, but more importantly, you will begin to understand yourself. I hope that if you did not share this experience with someone you will have the courage to do so later. You will find that it will help you enormously.

QUESTION TWO: TO TEACHERS AND OTHERS

Is the focus of your teaching:
1 teaching your subject specialism?
2 children's learning difficulties?
3 children's behaviour patterns?

Comments

1   If you focus on teaching your specialism and see your role as ensuring that all your children complete the curriculum, you will be creating severe discipline problems for yourself. Children are human beings and need to be recognised as such, not treated as material passing through a system. If they are to be motivated they need you to greet them as they enter the classroom, to give words of praise and encouragement to all—not forgetting those whom you would expect to be able to manage work on their own—and to show an interest in their personal affairs outside the classroom.

All children have the capacity to learn and you should see yourself as being there to make learning possible, not as an expert who is there only to impart knowledge—the latter is a bonus. If you take this approach you will find that it becomes considerably easier to motivate your pupils. The curriculum will be covered more effectively in that pupils will return your respect and work for you, rather than becoming bored with your subject-matter. When they are bored they will behave badly. The preparation of stimulating material will be to no avail unless you focus on each child's need for recognition.

EXERCISE ONE: TAKING A PERSONAL INTEREST
Write down the names of six pupils in your class and for each one list the following information (do not refer to anyone else):

Full name (include middle name):
Birthday:
Address:
Father's occupation:
Mother's occupation:
Names of brothers and sisters:
Other schools attended:
Closest school friend:
Favourite TV programme:
Favourite food:
Favourite football team:
Favourite pop star:
Main hobby:
Last holiday venue:
His ambition:

If you can provide most of this information, without having to refer to anyone, you will be approaching your teaching in the correct way. If you can provide little of the information, you will most likely be experiencing some difficulties. At the very least, you are not seeing your pupils working to their full potential.

You should find out personal background information by consulting previous teachers and by looking at the records of each incoming child. A good idea would be to note those who are having particular difficulties and to make the effort to find out more about their personal details. You should of course talk to all your pupils about themselves, but if you are restricted by time you should concentrate on those who have had problems and who would benefit from additional support.

Children in your group need you to take a personal interest in their lives, not simply to be there as some kind of mystical guru. The enthusiasm for your specialism is an important part of your appeal, but before the children can begin to learn they need you to see them as people.

2   If when you are teaching you focus on the difficulties that children may be experiencing, then you will be seeing yourself in the correct role. Given a good curriculum, stimulating material, an enthusiastic specialist, and someone who takes a genuine interest in their affairs, most pupils will still have difficulties in under-

standing certain concepts and processes. Not least the child with ADHD. You should see your role as being there to recognise this when it happens, not to complain when it does. Many teachers fall into the trap of thinking of pupils who are having difficulties as nuisances: things would somehow be different if only this or that child were not there. Those who are experienced know that as soon as one difficult child is removed from a group, another somehow emerges.

It is important to accept variation in all aspects of performance, and to reject the notion that all children are capable of performing at the same level. You will find that if you focus on the notion of natural variation and accept in a non-judgemental way that some will always have more difficulties than others, you will minimise the possibility of any behavioural problems.

EXERCISE TWO: FOCUSING ON LEARNING DIFFICULTIES
Take the bottom three names from a class list and complete the following for each:

Name:
1 Learning style:
2 Areas of weakness:
3 Areas of strength:

The more detailed the assessment you were able to give, the more evident is your interest in learning difficulties. If you are keeping accurate records you will have a good idea of the capabilities of each child and be able to expand on the details required in the above exercise. It is when you are ignorant of a child's capabilities that your level of expectation is unreasonable. A child with ADHD will find it difficult to cope with failure, and will react defensively if he feels threatened in this way. It is vital, therefore, to be aware of his attainment levels and to set work which can give him a chance to succeed.

If you are truly concentrating on the learning difficulties of a child, you will be keeping an accurate and up-to-date record of his performance and highlighting areas where difficulty is being experienced.

3 If you focus on the behaviour patterns of your children you

will find that they are linked to his learning processes. If a child is becoming frustrated because he cannot understand something, he will be unsettled and will start to misbehave. He will fool around with his classmates and do all he can to disrupt the proceedings.

A child with ADHD is restless to begin with and will be unable to retain information because of his incapacity to concentrate and his impulsive tendencies. Although he may be intelligent he may be unable to build on retained knowledge. He will be anxious because of this and supersensitive to criticism. Negative experiences in certain subject areas may have created learning blocks in him, and he will need a special approach to overcome them. Part of this approach would be the personal interest shown in him by his teacher: most learning difficulties and associated behavioural problems are caused, at least in part, by emotional insecurity, and a child with ADHD is particularly susceptible to this.

If you see your role as a keen observer of behaviour you will be able to prevent most of the disruption in the classroom which would come from a child with ADHD (see Chapter 9). The longer a child can go without letting himself down with his behaviour, the more chance there is of increasing his self-esteem—and of his good behaviour reinforcing itself. Seeing a child's behaviour as an indicator of his learning processes is therefore a very important part of teaching.

It is equally important to see his behaviour as a possible reflection of your own. In Question One the point was made to parents that it is vital to be honest about the contribution they might be making to a child's behaviour. If you are disorganised and chaotic, or if you are impulsive and unpredictable, then you will promote the same attitude in your pupils. Children will tend to imitate those facets of your style which are an inherent part of their own makeup.

If you are firm and fair in your controls, and if you combine this with a genuine interest not only in the work of the children, but also in their lives, then you will truly motivate them. They will present you with few behavioural problems.

The child with ADHD will need your special attention and concern for his personal life. Part of your interest will be the acknowledgement that he has this condition. How you approach this will need careful consideration, not least because of the reasons mentioned in Chapter 4. We shall discuss this in Chapter 9.

EXERCISE THREE: FOCUSING ON BEHAVIOURAL DIFFICULTIES

A   Take a class list and for each pupil complete the following:

1   Name:
2   Behaviour (one-word description):
3   Degree of consistency in this behaviour:
         always:
         periodically:
         specifically when:
         specifically when not:

B   Name the child who causes you most concern:

1   State his principal behavioural characteristic:
2   Describe the worst thing he has ever done:
3   Describe the worst thing he could possibly do:

You may be surprised at the descriptions you gave and at how difficult it was to describe the behaviour of some children. You should give more attention to those children whom you described rather blandly. It is these middle-of-the-road children who tend to be forgotten, and they will become bored and demotivated unless you attach special importance to them.

On completing this exercise you may have realised that the behaviour of most children is consistent. In a way this is a good sign, especially if they are consistently well-behaved and appear to be happy. However, if their behaviour is consistently of concern to you, you should examine whether you have given enough attention to the matters described in this chapter. If you feel that you have given the child due attention and that you have made special allowances for any problems indicated in his test data, then you must refer to a specialist: the child could have ADHD and be in need of professional help.

Do remember the central premises of this book—that the biological origins of behaviour should not be denied: when you are perplexed by a child's behaviour, and nothing you do seems to work, you should not hesitate to recommend that he be examined by a doctor. You are able to do this at Stage One of the Code of Practice (Appendix B). A child with ADHD may only respond to your work with the help of medication, and if you struggle on in the hope that one day he will change you may be deluding yourself. In the process you will also be doing him more harm than good and will be increasing the risk of disruptive behaviour among all your pupils.

It is useful to write down precisely what it is that concerns you about a child. Noting the worst thing he has ever done, and asking yourself what would be the worst thing that he could do, can often help your relationship. After you have asked these questions you are able to put things into perspective and you will feel less threatened by him.

QUESTION THREE: TO PARENTS AND PROFESSIONALS

Focusing on your feelings

When the child at the centre of your concern misbehaves do you feel:

1 emotionally involved?
2 out of control?
3 ashamed and incompetent?

Comments

1 Parents in particular become emotionally involved when their child misbehaves. It would be worrying if they did not, since it would imply that there was little bonding between them. Professionals likewise find it difficult to control their automatic response to a difficult child. However, it is important for you all to appreciate that you will only promote difficult behaviour by reacting to it in an emotional manner.

A child with ADHD is often emotionally fragile and finds it difficult to respond to people in a straightforward way. From an early age she may have felt a need to defend herself; over a period of time she will have begun to relate negatively to others. When you meet a child with ADHD you may thus be faced with a rather hostile way of interacting. If you reciprocate you will only make her condition worse.

You should not feel guilty about reacting to the child on an emotional level but you must be aware of the dangers of becoming involved in her emotional dynamics. A good idea is to imagine yourself wearing a white coat: you are a professional in charge of a case. You need to look at all the facts objectively.

It is difficult for parents to remain detached and it is for this reason that the family is not always the most appropriate setting for the child with ADHD (see Chapter 5).

2   If you feel out of control when dealing with a difficult child you should first look at yourself. Parents have already done this in Question One and I would refer professionals to that section.

It is of crucial importance that the child with ADHD be placed in a controlled and a controlling environment (see Chapter 7). If you are not strong enough to provide this, do not see it as a reflection of incompetence and feel guilty about it. Remember that we are all on a curve of natural variation and have different strengths and weaknesses: the important thing is to be honest about these. Schools and children's homes can only operate safely and efficiently if staff are open about each other's capabilities. If staff do not declare their weaknesses they cannot be given support, and the children will suffer the consequences.

If you are not clear about the controls you should be using you should consult the head of your school or home. A document outlining the control policy should be available. Children are protected by law from controls which may be construed as being abusive and against their rights (Appendix B).

3   If you feel ashamed when a child misbehaves, you have either a distorted perception of your role or the wrong perception of the child's condition.

Teachers and child careworkers often thing that everyone expects them to have perfect control over their charges from morning until night. They feel ashamed and humiliated when a child misbehaves, even when her condition is acknowledged, but they should not—unless they know that they have been negligent.

Because of the variable nature of the human condition it is not possible to predict all behaviour; difficulties will occur despite the very best preparation. You should therefore appreciate that crises are expected; you should not be in the business of hiding them or your fear of them.

If your perception of the child is that she is disabled, that she has the condition ADHD and probably has associated emotional and behavioural difficulties, then you will not be ashamed or humiliated when her condition becomes apparent. It is a feature of our society that it accords stigma to disablement; it is even more deplorable that it rejects disablement when there is no visual evidence immediately available. As a professional you should not share the same prejudices.

CONCLUSION

Parents and professionals dealing with children who have the condition ADHD are usually exhausted. At the beginning of the day the parent may have been woken well before the majority of us have begun to surface; her impulsive, hyperactive child may have been running about the house shouting, making demands, threatening. She may rise to this and fall asleep to it late every evening.

On weekdays the child's teacher may wake with an unsettled stomach which becomes progressively worse as school approaches. She may spend the day living on a knife edge, wondering how she will cope with the next episode of disruption. She may spend her evening avoiding rest and promoting nervous exhaustion in order that she can prepare work to keep the child occupied the next day. It is hard for outsiders to imagine the stress under which parents and professionals live and work when they are dealing with a child who has ADHD.

By looking at the way you think about your child, and how you think about yourself, you may have been able to put your personal situation into perspective. If you are a parent of a child with ADHD I hope you can recognise that before you can help your child you need to be a strong person in your own right. You need to have your own personal interests; you need to be separate from her and in a position of control. If you are a professional I hope that you can regard children as your speciality. In particular I hope that you can focus on their individual traits and performance characteristics. If you can do this you will be a first rate teacher of your subject specialism.

By making these kinds of adjustment to your attitude, and with the help of medication for your child, it may be possible to survive her behaviour. Later we shall be looking in more detail at what can be done in both the home and the school (Chapters 8 and 9). Although some questions in this chapter were addressed separately to parents and teachers, my hope is that you will read them all and consider the comments. If parents and professionals can understand the pressures that the child with ADHD brings to each of them, they will be able to devise a very effective programme of mutual support (see Chapter 10).

7   How Can I Help my Child?

If a child's behaviour is causing you and his teacher serious concern you should not hesitate to take him to the doctor. You have nothing to lose from this: should he be given a full diagnostic examination by a paediatrician you will learn, as precisely as anyone can, what aspects of his behaviour are a problem for you. You will be advised what can be done and given professional support.

After consultation with yourself and any professionals such as teachers who may be involved with your child, the specialist may diagnose ADHD. If he does he will prescribe a comprehensive treatment package, the aim of which will be to provide the optimum setting for the achievement of your child's full potential. ADHD cannot be cured: all that can be done is to minimise the development of unwanted secondary behavioural characteristics.

We have discussed how a child with ADHD is unable to concentrate and how he is at the mercy of his impulses. If such a child is not understood his behaviour will be condemned by those around him. He will be rejected by his peers and by adults and will quickly assume a negative self-image. He will feel threatened and behave more and more defensively as he strives to assert himself. He may react aggressively and attack people either verbally or physically, or he may cut himself off and retreat into the safety of his private fantasy world. His behaviour may appear bizarre and inexplicable.

The paediatrician may decide that your child does not have ADHD, but will still recommend a full treatment programme. This programme may or may not involve your child taking medication. It will, however, probably include other similar components, since, as I have already stated, the nature of any treatment programme is not to cure but to acknowledge and control. It may be possible for a child to be fully controlled by medication alone, but if he were he would be unable to relate to others, to think and to learn: he would be a vegetable. Paediatricians do not therefore simply prescribe drugs for children who have behavioural problems: they clearly see medication as only one component of a fully considered treatment programme.

In this chapter we shall examine in general terms how you can provide some elements of treatment which are a prerequisite for the effective use of medication. Whether your child has ADHD or not, you will find that his behaviour improves considerably if you give these matters serious consideration.

PROVIDING A SAFE ENVIRONMENT

A child with ADHD needs a setting that makes him feel secure. He needs to know that someone is in charge of his life, that certain events are predictable and that certain people can be relied upon. He needs consistency, controls and discipline; all of which will make him feel less anxious and may prevent him from developing unwanted patterns of behaviour.

Although it is important to understand the child with ADHD, this does not mean that you should tolerate his unwanted behaviour. He needs you to be in charge, to make him feel safe.

Consistency
Consistency is often equated with fairness, and should your child imagine that you have not applied the given rules he will react negatively. You should not therefore turn a blind eye when he is misbehaving. Deal with the situation at once, otherwise the small crisis you have felt able to ignore will escalate into a major confrontation. The tiniest misdemeanour may appear trivial to you; to him it may be as significant as any other.

If you are working as part of a team you must adopt the same approach. If you see a child misbehaving behind one of your colleagues' backs, you need to take action. Staff who lead teams should tell their members to take this approach if the necessary degree of consistency is to be achieved. They should not see such an intervention as a threat to their professionalism; rather, it is a sign of their genuine commitment to dealing with the child's behaviour.

Likewise, both parents should deal with a child's misdemeanours in the same way. To do this requires the establishment of some guidelines: one could be that whoever makes a decision to deviate from previously agreed policies will not be questioned at all in the presence of the child; only when the child is out of earshot will matters be discussed. A second guideline could be that parents should not get hung up about the rightness of policies: the essential component is that they present a united approach. To achieve this a third guideline could be that parents will communicate with each other and accept that policies may from time to time be adjusted or simply forgotten by their partner.

The important thing to remember is that the total setting in which the child with ADHD exists, whether at home or at school, should as far as possible have a consistent philosophy and approach.

Activities and routines
It is important to prepare the day thoroughly for your child. Unlike other children, the child with ADHD needs someone to organise things around him in order that he can work and play; he finds his free time the hardest to manage.

If you are teaching him, provide a personal curriculum; if you do not he will not understand the work, will be unable to do it and will become more impulsive. It is of course important for him to learn to play, but this too must be scheduled as part of the daily routine. If specific activities are provided for him he will come to see it as a recognisable activity session and feel quite secure with it.

Parents, too, should plan each day carefully, dividing it up into recognisable periods during which different activities take place. This will help them to get through the day as much as it will help their child. The routines should be applied as consistently as possible throughout the week.

It is a good idea for both parents and professionals to plan out not only the week, but the term. This should not be done in detail, but significant events placed at strategic intervals can act not only as incentives and rewards but as permanent anchor points in the child's life. If he knows that every Easter he visits his grandmother, or that in the summer term he is allowed to look after the school weather station, it will add to his sense of security.

Built into his programme at home should be periods when a parent can go off on her own, either to rest or, more importantly, to pursue a personal hobby or pastime.

Being consistent does not imply that you should necessarily be blindly persistent in all you try to do with your child. Although the value of routines and activities is the sense of security they can promote, you should recognise the need to adjust them when it is clear that your child is not benefiting. Sometimes it works well if you inject something different into the daily schedule: it can be refreshing and enhance the value of your routine programme. However, do make sure that you are the one who decides when to do this, and that you do not do it so regularly that your routine either changes or disappears.

Consequences and controls

The child with ADHD often presents as lively, imaginative and full of intelligence. Parents and professionals see him as a small person with enormous potential. They cater to his every whim and rush around trying to satisfy his boundless energy and curiosity. They have a genius on their hands; all he needs is constant stimulation and he will begin to settle. Accordingly they dedicate their lives to meeting his needs and tolerate the moments when they feel totally drained and exhausted. The child is at the centre of their lives—and in full control: he leads and they follow.

By doing so, and with the best intentions possible, they deny him his most basic right. Every child has a right to feel that someone else is in charge of his life: he needs this before he can begin to grow towards a sense of being in control of himself.

You may feel that your child is completely out of control. In Chapter 6 we looked at your first course of action: you must begin to feel stronger, to control yourself. To do this you must look inwards and share your thoughts and feelings with others, and then look at the practical way in which you can help your child in the home and the school (Chapters 8 and 9).

Later in this chapter we shall see how you can begin to control your child by using language more effectively, and by recognising the need to develop communication skills. It may be your experience, however, that he can use language very effectively. Using a level of articulation that you might interpret as charm, or admire as a sign of his undoubted intelligence, he tends to control you, rather than you him. You may have discussed his behaviour with him many times, to no effect. Information seems to go in one ear and out the other. If he does as you say one moment, when the same situation recurs, ten minutes later, he has seemingly decided to ignore your instructions.

You realise of course that a child with ADHD has a genuine difficulty in this respect; but he may still benefit from feeling the consequences of his actions. If he hits his brother and you verbally admonish him, he may stop what he is doing, but the next time his brother frustrates him he is likely to hit him again, more especially if you are not there. If you want your message to stick, instead of making a huge verbal issue of the matter you should calmly tell him of your disapproval. Soon after, when he is expecting some goodie, such as watching his favourite TV programme, you should cancel it.

Do not attempt to explain or excuse your actions, other than to say that you might have allowed him to watch it if he had not hit his brother. Avoid saying more than this, otherwise he will imagine that your decision is open to negotiation. This course of action may be difficult to take, but it will have the desired effect of driving home a twofold message: firstly, that he is not to hit his brother; secondly, that you are in charge.

I repeat that you should not open the matter to discussion. Take action calmly at the time of the event in order to prevent harm coming to anyone; later, follow it with a consequence. You can shout at your child for ever and all you will be doing is teaching him how to shout. If you have the strength quietly to take the action recommended above, you will help him to become calm and controlled. Remember the old saying 'actions speak louder than words'. His impulsive, uncontrolled actions should tell you that he is falling apart; your quiet but firm approach should assure him of your strength.

Before you can use this approach you must be in a position where you are offering the child a great deal. If you offer no goodies, then in the event that you wish to face him with a consequence, you will have nothing to withdraw. Indeed, if you offer him nothing pleasurable he will simply not do anything you suggest. He needs to know that you are investing in him before he will pay attention to what you say.

Make sure, therefore, that in the plan for each day there is a special treat, that there is a goodie in store for each week, and that there are significant carrots in the long term. Do not use these as threats in any way. Make sure that the child knows of them but do not threaten to withdraw them. When you withdraw goodies it must be done to effect and be directly related to a misdemeanour that has occurred in the recent past. The medium and long term carrots should therefore never be touched, but merely mentioned and left to dangle in the child's mind. The daily treats should be the ones that are withdrawn when sanctions are required.

There are other actions you can take and we shall consider these in a moment, but before doing so we need to look at the measures you should never take.

Unacceptable consequences

Children have rights and it is important to know that the following actions would be deemed unacceptable by those who protect them in law.

a CORPORAL PUNISHMENT

Corporal punishment is defined as the intentional application of force as punishment. You are not allowed to slap, push or punch a child as a response to his behaviour.

If you are a professional you should be aware that any action involving physical punishment is unacceptable. You are allowed to take physical action which may avert the possibility of immediate danger or personal injury to the child, others, yourself or property, but any force used must be moderate and reasonable. You are allowed to hold or restrain a child for these purposes.

b DEPRIVATION OF FOOD AND DRINK

A child should never be denied access to the range of food and drink normally available. Mealtime consequences should therefore always allow for the normal intake of food.

c   DENIAL OF ACCESS TO PARENTS OR RELATIVES
If you are a professional you should plan the visits a parent might make to your child. You should recognise the need the child will always have for regular contact with his natural home. You should never restrict his access to his parents or relatives as a punishment.

d   USE OF ACCOMMODATION TO RESTRICT LIBERTY
Professionals are allowed to make sure that a child's accommodation is safe and secure from intruders. They are also allowed to keep him on premises when they have calculated that he will be a danger to himself or others. They should never confine him to accommodation as punishment.

e   INTENTIONAL DEPRIVATION OF SLEEP
A child should never be denied sleep. If he is awake and unable to sleep he may be removed from a bedroom or dormitory in order that others may sleep, but only until such time as he himself is ready to do so. He should not be stood in a corridor or subjected to physical activities in an attempt to tire him out.

f   FINES
Fines should never be used as punishment for unacceptable behaviour, although a child may be fined in order that property can be repaired or replaced.

g   INTIMATE PHYSICAL SEARCHES
You may search a child's clothes, but this should never be done as a punishment, only ever as a safety measure. You are *never* allowed to search his body.

h   THE USE OR WITHHOLDING OF MEDICATION OR MEDICAL
TREATMENT, INCLUDING DENTISTRY
You should never deny a child access to any medical treatment.

It may seem unnecessary to state these unacceptable consequences. However, if you think carefully about your present practices, you may be surprised at how close you come to violating the child's rights. If you are an adult responsible for a child with ADHD, it could be said that you would be guilty of this if you did not, for example, see that he regularly attended the dentist's, and you would have a clear duty to administer Ritalin if a doctor has prescribed it.

Acceptable consequences

Rather than thinking punitively, you should develop a system of rewards and incentives which are related to activities that the child may share with you and others. You should concentrate on praising him and extending his privileges when he behaves well. If you do not bear these two points in mind, then no matter what consequences you devise for him, you will find that they have little lasting value. In devising your consequences you could use the following sanctions:

a SUSPEND LEISURE ACTIVITIES
See previous discussion, pp. 114–15.

b EXTRA WORK
Give him the opportunity to make up by doing work, but never use school work for this purpose as you will only encourage his dislike of it. Use instead chores around the house or classroom. Choose chores that he will be able to do and which will not take him too long. Bear in mind that the child with ADHD has great difficulty in staying on task and that if you give him work that takes a long time you may be promoting more problems. If necessary supervise him closely: you will then be able to tell when he has reached his limit. Extra work should be for some constructive purpose and for the benefit of others: in this way you will give the child an opportunity to assuage himself, to achieve and to experience the pleasure associated with helping others.

Consequences should be applied as soon as possible after the misdemeanour. With this and the above points in mind, here are some basic guidelines:

1   Have five carefully planned main work consequences available for instant use.
2   Have five carefully planned secondary consequences to which you can quickly transfer if your child is clearly finding the first task beyond him.

3   Make sure that it is you and not he who makes the decision to terminate the task or to transfer.

4   Be positive rather than punitive in your approach.

5   Praise him for a job well done.

If you take this approach you may find that after a while your child self-monitors his behaviour: when he is unable to cope with those around him he may make the decision to do one of the work consequences. To enable him to do this you should have equipment and materials available for at least one consequence.

c   EARLY BED

Do not send your child to bed too early: doing this could lead to further problems. Your impulsive, hyperactive child may find it difficult to stay in bed anyway, and going to bed early could mean as little as five or ten minutes. If you have regularly defined and consistent schedules this gesture could have great potency.

d   SEND HIM TO HIS ROOM OR TO A QUIET AREA

If you do this, make sure that it is equipped properly (see Chapter 8). The consequence time can then be used constructively, and your child may turn to this as a technique to avoid situations which prove too much for him. The strategy may give him an opportunity to develop another self-monitoring skill, and provide him with a 'release valve' for those times when he is aware of letting himself down in the eyes of others.

e   SUSPEND PRIVILEGES

Whether the child is at home or at school he should be given small privileges. These will give him a sense of responsibility. He will relish them and regret it if they are withdrawn.

It is important to project to a child that sanctions are punishments, but in your own mind try to look at them positively, as opportunities for restitution and 'clearing the slate'; be creative and imagine how you can put them to good use.

Rewards

The child with ADHD needs to have his day fully organised for him. He should have a regular routine which can provide him with a sense of safety and security, and this should be interspersed with built-in incentives. Regular enjoyable activities which the child can successfully manage must be a feature of each day if you want him to respond positively to your controls (see Discipline, below). These may be withdrawn as sanctions, but you should focus on rewards rather than punishment. To do this you will need to look for the times when your child is behaving appropriately.

Most of us tend to pay more attention to a child when he is behaving badly; when he is quiet and controlled we tend to keep away from him in case we break the spell. Regrettably, by doing this we are reinforcing the very behaviour we wish to extinguish.

When your child is behaving well, quietly join him and give him an encouraging word. Do not press into his personal space if it is clear that he wants to be left alone, but when you can, try to reinforce his behaviour with your attention. You could quietly reward him by allowing him to perform a small task that you know he enjoys, or by giving him some of his favourite food. You should do this intermittently—that is, not on a regular basis. The idea is that he should not expect the reward. This will prevent him from turning the process into a game which he could manipulate to his advantage. Rather, on a subconscious level he will begin to associate the intermittent rewards with appropriate behaviour, and this will be internalised.

Discipline

Discipline is important for all children since it implies that there are boundaries for behaviour, a shape to existence. It gives meaning to life and promotes personal strength; it creates a sense of security and self-determination.

Parents tend to impose their own experience of discipline on their child and it is perhaps significant that those with problem children exert few controls. Children in these families spend a great deal of time out of sight of their parents; their behaviour is not monitored and controlled. Their parents often do not know where they are or what they are doing. Children with conduct disorders (Chapter 2) see their parents as unable to set limits to

their behaviour. They receive no explicit guidance on how
to behave and their parents tend to avoid any matters that may
lead to confrontation. When problems do arise the parents may
shout and gesticulate, but fail to follow the matter through with
sanctions.

This style of discipline transmits a message of rejection to the
child: it appears to him that his parents do not care what he does.
It is often ineffective because it is a reflection of the parent's mood
rather than the child's behaviour.

Discipline involves arriving at solutions to problems and
families with difficult children are usually unable to make
decisions; any discipline therefore tends to be both negative and
diffuse. Children will only comply with the requests of adults
whom they respect. Discipline is achieved in families which have
shared positive experiences, but in families with difficult children
these are sadly lacking.

We all recognise that children need discipline. The hard part is
the practical implementation. If we control too heavily and refuse
to listen to anything the child may say, we promote a lack of
conscience, low self-esteem and social withdrawal. We may even
promote stealing and lying. If we are indulgent or permissive we
may promote the child's impulsivity. If we are indifferent to his
behaviour, and take no notice of it, we are again promoting a
sense of insecurity and low self-esteem.

If, however, we are able to combine firm and clear rule-setting
with a pleasant form of interaction with the child, we shall promote
within him both the sense of security that comes from external
control and the sense of personal worth that comes from increased
responsibility. Because of his innate tendency to distractibility,
impulsivity and hyperactivity, the child with ADHD needs a safe
environment: he needs to feel that someone is in control and has
a level of expectations just above his reach. In this respect discipline can be the breath of life to him, but only if it is accompanied
by enjoyable shared experiences (see Rewards, above).

Here are some simple but important guidelines for disciplining
your child:

A   Before your child will respond to discipline in a meaningful
way you will need to spend time with him sharing mutually enjoy-

able experiences. If you do nothing with ↦
to conform, you may see him do so but i↦
not respect. His conformity will be tempora↦
exist when you are not there. Check to see t↦
every effort to do things with your child. Be↦
difficult behaviour you may have stopped doing↦
he may never seem to appreciate your efforts, o↦   ↦
embarrassment to you (see Chapter 6). It is import↦   ↦wever,
for you to continue with the positive side of your relat↦onship with
him if you want him to respond to your discipline.

B   Use rewards effectively (see Rewards, above):
1   Focus on rewards rather than punishments.
2   Pre-plan meaningful rewards.
3   Seize every opportunity to praise and encourage.

c   Use consequences effectively:
1   Pre-plan effective consequences.
2   Remain calm and clearly state what the child has done: do not
    debate the issue.
3   Administer the consequence immediately.
4   Be prepared to supervise the consequence.
5   Praise him when he has fulfilled the consequence.

COMMUNICATING

In Chapter 5 I mentioned why children react negatively:

1   when they cannot get their own way;
2   when they feel as though they are being criticised;
3   when they think that they are being treated unfairly.

You can avoid these situations and minimise the possibility of
unwanted behaviour from your child by focusing on the need to
communicate clearly with him.

Clarify your plans

At the beginning of every day or lesson, choose a time when you
can speak to him on his own. It is important to speak to him in
private: he will not be distracted by others and able to play to

owd, and he will benefit from this small dose of personal attention.

Mention to him what you will be doing. Do not speak harshly but be quiet, clear and firm. Do not leave it open to discussion. Clearly, if you were to do this you would not be providing him with the controls that he so desperately needs.

If he objects and becomes loud, remain calm and simply restate the plan. Leave him and make sure that you do something else: it is important for you to project to him that his objections are not at the centre of your concern. If you stand there pleading with him to comply with your wishes, he will become more confused. When you return to him you should project an assumption that he is ready to begin and start your programme positively.

If he complies, do not make such an issue of this that you give him ammunition for the future, but later, when he is doing what you wish and when he perhaps does not expect it, make sure that you provide him with extra doses of encouragement (see Rewards, above). If he does not comply, leave him where he is for a while and put your thinking cap on! A guiding principle is that you and not he should be in control.

You could therefore quickly manipulate the situation to this end. For example, if you are a parent and have explained the plan for the morning and your child is still refusing to go shopping, you could put your coat on and make all final preparations. You could find, as you checked the back garden gate, that it was wide open. You could return to your child and express surprise, asking whether he heard anyone in the night and would he come and check for clues? You could ask him to look round the house and to secure all windows and so on. You could then casually tell him to get his coat on. You would gauge very carefully how long you took on the 'investigation'. Too little and he would not have snapped out of his game of opposition, too late and he would lose his sense of new-found comradeship with you.

If you are a professional you should adopt a similar approach, and use all the resources at your disposal to communicate and control (see Chapter 9).

Express yourself and your child
A child with ADHD will often misinterpret the message he receives from others: he finds it difficult to focus and his impulsivity will make him react without forethought to what you say. Secondary characteristics will have developed from the ADHD and in particular a low level of self-esteem: he will be very sensitive to the slightest thing you say and you will need to consider carefully the way in which you communicate with him.

Expressing yourself
Here are some guidelines:

1   Always try to speak to him on his own when you have something important to say.
2   Before you speak make sure that he is in one of his calm periods.
3   Speak to him quietly but firmly: appear confident.
4   Never make threats (see Consequences and Controls, above).
5   Repeat the same message in at least four ways, culminating in your original statement.

Expressing the child
You should also help your child to express himself. Although a child with ADHD may often be articulate, it is important to do all you can to encourage him to express his feelings. He may not be able to do this verbally, and you should provide opportunities for him to do so in a non-verbal way: drawing, modelling and acting are ways of doing this, and computing can help the child who has particular difficulty in acquiring basic literacy skills. During activity sessions, whether he be a five-year-old doing his clay-modelling or a teenager on his computer, you could begin to talk to him about what he is doing and gradually improve his ability to express his feelings.

In both the home and the school, therefore, you should provide materials and equipment for this purpose (see Chapters 8 and 9).

Listen
When your child begins to express his feelings you should regard yourself as a listener. Do not be tempted to prod and probe into

his past; be wary of putting things into his mouth; do not start to tell him what he could have done, and make a special effort never to use the word 'should'.

Provide a sympathetic ear only. A great deal of harm is done to children by parents and professionals who promote introspection. Children should be living their lives, not talking about them. They must be allowed to go at their own pace when it comes to looking at their past. The child has to feel his way into an understanding of himself, and you must appreciate that as an adult you will be capable of recognising feelings and dynamics that he cannot. If you project these onto him you will be doing him a great deal of harm; he will adopt psychological and behavioural models in his mind that will have no basis in either his intellect or his emotions. Allow the child to express himself, do not drift into using the opening as an opportunity to express yourself.

We shall discuss how you might encourage your child talk less and listen more in Chapters 8 and 9.

STRENGTHENING

Before we begin to discuss in more detail the practical measures that you can employ in the home and classroom, it would be useful to take a final look at some basic principles which might underlie your work.

When you are involved in dealing with difficult children you must adopt a highly imaginative and personal approach, and to be able to do this you need to be sure of your long-term aims and objectives. If you are not, your work will suffer from a lack of substance and you will quickly lose a sense of direction. Time spent with the child, whether as a parent or a teacher, will become more meaningful, and bearable, for you if you are able to look upon it as part of a theme.

Your child's distractibility, impulsivity and hyperactivity could form the basis for your programme but we shall be looking at how you might deal with these later. To conclude this chapter I would like you to consider another approach which focuses on the basic needs we all have, and from which not only your child, but you yourself could benefit.

Personal assessment

A central aim in your work with all children should be the creation of a strong sense of personal identity. The child who is presenting behavioural problems will undoubtedly think little of himself: you should focus on improving his self-esteem, and to begin with you should help him to clarify exactly who he is and what his life is composed of. You should not begin by dealing with his past, but should concentrate on the present.

Help him in whatever way you can to acknowledge the people who are most important to him, the places that are meaningful and the significant events that he regularly looks forward to. Discuss his personal appearance and his likes and dislikes; consider his network of friends and relatives and how he spends his time. Your aim should be to encourage him to look at his life objectively and to resolve any of the ambivalent feelings he may have. A constant objective should always be the raising of his self-esteem.

Achieving a sense of identity is a continuous process for all of us, but when you are dealing with a child who has ADHD you must make a conscious effort to help him develop a clear image. His distractibility may have prevented him from building a picture of himself. Moreover, when you are talking to him you will be able to counterbalance the inevitable negative feelings he has about himself.

If you help your child towards a positive assessment of himself you will be strengthening him. If he feels strong he will react less defensively. Part of this assessment should be the explanation of ADHD.

If you make your child feel stronger in himself, and if you explain his condition correctly, you will be promoting self-control.

Personal discipline

If you want to help your child achieve a positive sense of identity and personal control you should recognise the valuable part that personal discipline and will-power can play. We all know that unless we are stretched in some way we cannot feel our limitations, and that if there is no level of expectation we do not experience achievement. When we lose our will-power we become depressed, resentful and confused; we feel helpless, controlled by the world around us.

A sense of personal power and control can come through disciplined exercise, whereby a child might channel and develop his will-power in a positive way. Encourage him to do something, on a daily basis, that stretches him and can become a regular part of his schedule. Physical exercise is particularly useful since it is known to produce physiological change conducive to a sense of calmness and well-being; if a regular schedule is adhered to, this in itself promotes a sense of order and harmony. Discipline in any sphere of activity could benefit the child with ADHD, but not if its demands are beyond his capabilities, so if you introduce a schedule of discipline use the following guidelines:

1 Make sure the task is within his reach.
2 Be prepared to accompany him in order to encourage him and to gauge its appropriateness.
3 Introduce a clear system of rewards and incentives.

If possible you should try to include another child. You will need to make sure that each has appropriate individual targets—do not make it into a competition. If you approach it properly this could be one way of helping your child to make a friend.

Personal heroes
The child with ADHD may be fully aware of what he would like to be and what he would like to do, but he may experience severe frustration in achieving his aims. His desire to make friends could be a good example. We all experience frustration in this respect: we have our idea of what the perfect person, place or event should be, and although it is necessary to have these images in our mind, when they cause excessive frustration they should be broken and replaced with more attainable ideals.

By looking at your child's ideal models it may be possible for him to come to a realistic appraisal of what he might like to be, how he might like to appear to others. It might enable him to see how others presently perceive him and how they might like him to be.

Personal control
When the child is strong enough, when his sense of identity and wholesomeness is crystallised, we can move him to the final stage where he may begin to achieve personal control. This involves

helping him to separate his condition from himself. He must come to appreciate that he is separate from his distractibility, impulsivity and hyperactivity, that he is apart from ADHD and in a position of control. It is only when he totally identifies with his condition that he is subjected to its vacillations.

If he can look at his condition objectively and develop the ability to dissociate from it, then he will be able to cope with it rather than suffer from it. He will be able to accept himself for what he is and develop the ability to make adjustments to his behaviour. However, he will abuse this approach if it is premature and will take every advantage of a situation where he is not responsible for his actions. Whenever he is in trouble, he will simply blame ADHD. You must make sure that the first three stages have achieved their objectives before moving to the fourth: be aware that it may take many months or even years before you can do this. You will be able to tell whether a child is ready to begin this stage by his degree of self-confidence and realism.

If you are to implement this particular programme, or any other, you should be aware of the need to be covert in your action with a child. If you openly state what you are trying to do, he will play the game and string along with you. Your whole programme could become a charade, and of no lasting value. You must always work to your private aim and within your previously defined parameters; he should be allowed to benefit through the exercises you devise for him.

These four principles should thread their way through your work. Children with ADHD invariably develop low self-esteem and need a programme of personal strengthening. When they are stronger in themselves they are able to look at their condition objectively and begin to adjust to it. If these principles underpin any techniques which you employ you can guarantee that you will be going in the right direction.

CONCLUSION

When you are wondering what you can do to help your child you should begin by asking what you are trying to achieve. My presumption would be that you would like your child to be more able to stay on task, to be less impulsive and restless—in short, to be more in control of himself. You can help him do this by creating an environment which, because of its consistency and reliability, will give him a sense of security: you can create a setting where there are expectations, consequences and rewards for behaviour; you can adjust the way you speak to him so that what you say is clear and unequivocal; you can listen to what he says and provide a sympathetic ear. All of this will give him the feeling that he is safe, that someone else is in control.

If you can help him to know who he is and to identify the significant people, places and events in his life, you will be leading him to a position of personal control. By encouraging him to take part in disciplined physical exercise you may help him to feel the boundaries of his self; by discussing his ideal world and his heroes you may be able to diminish his sense of failure and frustration.

Finally, if after many months or even years and when he is strong enough, you can begin to encourage him to feel separate from his condition and his feelings, you will be giving him the key to the rest of his life. You will not have cured his condition, but you will have put him fully in charge of it, and of his own destiny.

8   What Can be Done in the Home?

It is hard for those who do not have to deal with a difficult child to appreciate the enormous stress that he places on his parents. Even professionals who work with the child may not fully understand what it is like to live with him: teachers in mainstream schools only see the child for limited periods of time; those who deal with him in residential settings usually work split shifts and are able to regard him as part of a small group rather than an individual. Whatever their level of contact with the child, professionals can at the end of the day walk away from him: if they are properly trained they can look at him in a detached and controlled manner.

Ideally parents should try to separate themselves from their child; they should aim to become stronger and more objective in their approach to him (see Chapter 6). However, this is easier said than done. Living on a permanent basis with a child who has ADHD can be physically and mentally exhausting and can drive a parent towards a nervous breakdown.

If you are a professional you should realise this and focus on supporting the parent rather than condemning her. If she appears incapable of dealing with her child, ask yourself the following questions:

1   How much do you know about her personal situation?
2   Do you think that she enjoys her predicament?
3   If you were in her position, would criticism help you or make your situation worse?

We shall be looking in Chapter 10 at the ways in which professionals may support families with difficult children, but I emphasise the importance of this now because I want parents to realise that experts recognise that the most effective way of helping difficult children is to help their parents.

If you are a parent you should realise that those who specialise in these matters know how you suffer: they appreciate that having a child with ADHD can place enormous stress on you and other members of your family; they acknowledge that your child has been born with a condition which is hard for you to live with; they know that you cannot be held responsible for his behaviour.

You yourself may find this hard to accept because of the emphasis which our society places on the effect of an environment on a child's behaviour; you may continue to feel guilty about the way you have raised your child. If you want to make a fresh start and if you want a future you will need to think differently. Accept the fact that all children have their own personal characteristics when they are born: they do not arrive with a completely clean slate on which you write their future. Should your child have ADHD he was distractible, impulsive and hyperactive at birth.

This does not mean that there is nothing you can do to help him. To begin with you should try to understand his condition by reading Part One of this book, and then you should consider how you can create the best possible environment for him. We began to do this in Chapter 6 where I suggested that both parents and professionals should examine their attitude to the difficult child; we continued in Chapter 7 by looking at ways in which you might provide a setting which would give your child a sense of security, and we discussed a long-term programme that might help him to feel stronger within himself and more able to cope with his condition. In this chapter we shall focus on how the child might be helped in the home situation. Professionals will find the suggestions useful points for discussion when they are attempting to support parents.

LOOK FOR HELP

If you are seriously concerned about your child's behaviour you should seek help. Do not struggle on regardless, feeling that if you tell people of the difficulty you are having with your child they will only blame you.

Teacher

If your child attends school, speak to his teacher about your concerns—teachers are there to help and understand. If you are concerned about your child you can guarantee that his teacher will already be aware that he has problems; she will welcome a visit from you since the information you give her will help her to form a plan of action.

Do not hesitate to do this when your child is very young: often parents feel that children grow out of difficult behaviour, but while this may be true for most, the behaviour of children with ADHD will worsen unless it is acknowledged and treated.

Your child's teacher will be able to discuss his behaviour with you and work out strategies which you can employ; if these fail she may seek the advice of a specialist (see Appendix B: The Code of Practice). A special person is appointed in UK schools to make sure that the needs of those children who are experiencing difficulties are met. This person is the Special Educational Needs Co-ordinator. He or she will be involved at some stage in helping you and the classroom teacher to provide a suitable programme for your child.

Doctor/paediatrician/psychologist

When your child's behaviour suddenly changes, or when he is persistently difficult, you should take him to your doctor. Doctors are concerned with behaviour patterns since they often indicate medical problems, and as we saw in Chapter 2, it is the doctor who would refer your child to a paediatrician if he thought it appropriate.

The paediatrician will provide you not only with an analysis of your child's behaviour, but with a comprehensive treatment programme. This will detail adjustments which should be made at school and at home and may involve medication: medication on its own, however, would never be recommended. As part of his assessment the paediatrician will consult you yourself, teachers and other specialists such as psychologists who are experts in their own field.

Friends and neighbours

You should explain your child's behaviour to your close neighbours and friends: they too will have had to suffer from it. You should tell them how you see your child's problems and how you are trying to help him. If they understand how you feel and what you are trying to do they will help you. If you think that they will automatically know what is going on you can expect trouble. They need to be convinced that your child needs help: you can guarantee that at the moment they will regard him merely as a nuisance who needs either to be locked up or severely punished.

Begin by being honest about your feelings of guilt and failure; explain how you have consulted your child's teacher and doctor; describe ADHD. Tell them what has happened so far and how you are trying to help. Try to understand their viewpoint and resist becoming frustrated with their attitude. Focus on listening and sharing: they will eventually understand and will provide you with a source of practical help and moral support.

PROVIDE REASSURANCE

An escape route

Your child needs people other than yourself to whom he can relate and who can help him to feel more sure about who he is and what he stands for. He needs someone who is less attached to him, another relationship which is qualitatively different. You will find that if he has this other person he will often behave completely differently with him or her. His attitude to you will also change. It is often the case that if a child has the facility of an alternative relationship he will relax in his present one.

With an older child you should arrange for him to have somewhere to go when he is becoming restless with you. You will find that he will use this place according to his needs. Often the very fact that there is somewhere to go means that he is able to relax more in the home. When he feels trapped he will become more distractible, impulsive and hyperactive. Having another place for him to go can act as a safety valve not only for him but for yourself; because of his absence, and knowing where he is, you will have the opportunity to relax.

External groups

If it is impossible to recruit a neighbour or a friend who might provide this facility, you could search your locality for a group of some kind which he might join. You will need to explain his condition to those who are in charge and to kindle their enthusiasm. When you are discussing the viability of your child joining a group you should bear in mind the following:

a   Will he be able to stay on task long enough to meet their requirements?
b   If he cannot, could anything be done to make it possible for him to attend?
c   Is the level of supervision and support sufficient for his needs?

It would be a good idea to visit the group yourself beforehand so that you can answer these questions, and be prepared to provide assistance yourself, at least in the initial stages. Joining a group would give your child not only another safety valve but also a sense of belonging; if planned carefully it could help him to develop a stronger and more positive self-image.

A place of safety

Every child should have his own room. He needs a place which is his, which he can control and use to express himself. The child with ADHD in particular needs a place where he can get away from others, a private place where he has the opportunity to lie and do nothing; he is known only for his high level of activity and in public tends to live up to the expectations of others.

Regrettably, his room is more often than not associated with rejection. He is sent there when others can no longer tolerate his behaviour. You should avoid this by privately explaining that his room is where he can go when he feels that he is not coping with others. If this strategy is employed you will need to equip his room so that he has something to do when he gets there; he will be in and out again before you know where you are unless it has its attractions.

We all have our moments, and when these occur we either do nothing but try to get our thoughts together by lying still and closing our eyes, or we take our minds off things by doing something. If your child has a comfortable bed to lie on and if the room is equipped with alternative activities, then you will find that he will begin to put it to good use: when he feels himself losing control, he will look to the room as a safety valve—it will become a positive part of his repertoire.

When you equip his room for this purpose you should consider the appeal of computers to a child with ADHD. When he plays on a computer a child's ability to stay on task is often dramatically enhanced. Because he feels less threatened by others and because he can choose his own skill level he has a greater chance of experiencing success. A music facility can also be of great benefit to him. You should buy relaxation tapes and scatter them among his own for him to discover and use: Gregorian chant is thought by some to be therapeutic for such children. For your own sake do not forget to provide him with headphones!

Other equipment and materials such as a modelling kit, a railway layout, books, comics, drawing and writing materials should be provided according to his interests.

I would recommend, however, that there is only one television set in the house and that it is not in his room. Television is an extremely attractive and potent medium; it can be abused by children but can be a useful tool for passive gatherings of the family. In the face of the attractions which his pleasantly furnished room offers, it might be the only thing to tempt your child to join you from time to time!

You should not be worried if your son does spend a large part of his spare time in his room: because of his condition a child with ADHD finds it easier to cope on his own. If you can relax in the knowledge that to force him to do anything else with his time could create more problems for him, you will avoid making him feel abnormal.

You can of course affect how much time he spends in his room by the way in which you organise the remainder of his day for him and by offering him alternative attractions. If he has someone outside the home to visit when he is beginning to feel restless, and if you have planned regular routines and activities into his weekly schedule (see Chapter 7), the spare time he has to spend in his room should cause you no concern.

Keeping in touch

Whenever possible you should take the opportunity to provide your child with the warmth of physical contact. Often this is denied to a child who presents his parents only with worries and anxieties; the child then feels rejected and becomes unable to feel in contact with his parents; it seems impossible for them both to achieve any degree of closeness. However, there may be occasions when a hug and a cuddle are possible. You will know when this is the case and should take advantage of it.

You may find it difficult to express yourself in this way, but if you can look upon it as a need that your child has, you may be able to provide this very basic form of human contact for him. The child with ADHD will tend to operate at extremes: according to his impulses he will either shun physical contact or suffocate you with it.

If you find that he wants to be close do not resent it or, for convenience, push him away: recognise his need to be close to you; respect also the need he may have to resist contact. You should not interpret any of his behaviour as a rejection of yourself; simply accept that his feelings will vacillate, and be determined to remain available for contact should he need it. As well as physically reassuring your child you should show an interest in his hopes and aspirations and in whatever he is doing. Try to share his concerns and show that you care who he is. Take every opportunity to emphasise to him that while you may disapprove of his behaviour, you accept and love him.

Simply sitting with him when he is looking at a book and being quiet, or watching television and chatting, are signs that you are willing to spend time with him. Remember also that a dose of affection at the right time can reinforce his good behaviour.

An effective way of giving reassurance is by using humour. A well-timed humorous comment might be enough to spark something between you. It might indicate that you are on the same wavelength: it could tell him that you know where he is, how he is feeling. Be careful, however, not to use sarcasm or to be cynical—the risk of misinterpretation is too great. Be sure at all times that there is no condemnatory subscript to your humorous comment: if it is at all judgemental it will be far more hurtful to him than a simple statement.

By looking for ways in which you can give reassurance to your child you will strengthen him: he will become less defensive and more able to adapt to his condition.

TEACH HIM HOW TO BEHAVE

By the time most parents decide to ask for help, the behaviour of their child has driven them to the point where they are confused and bewildered: they do not know whether it is they who are getting everything wrong or their child. If they are asked to describe his behaviour they may find it impossible to begin.

If you are worried by your child's behaviour and find it difficult to put your finger on what it is that causes you concern, you may find it helpful to use the checklists in Chapter 2. Do bear in mind, however, that only a specialist will be able to make an accurate diagnosis of your child's condition: the checklists will be useful in that they may help you to decide whether your concerns could be justified. When you discuss his behaviour with either his teacher or a specialist, the lists will also help you to describe what he does more accurately.

Armed with an accurate description, teachers and other professionals will be able to discuss with you various ways in which together you might try to modify your child's behaviour. There are certain general guidelines:

Remain calm

Your child comes in from school. He throws his coat on the floor and kicks off his shoes. He ignores you when you speak to him and turns the television on loud. He swears at you when you ask what he would like for tea. He turns the television off and runs upstairs. He bangs his bedroom door hard. You hear him throwing furniture around and yelling obscene language at you. There is a crash and his door bangs again as he rushes downstairs and into the kitchen. When you ask him what he is doing he replies with foul language.

Your immediate reaction to him coming in like a tornado will be to control him, to stop him physically. You will feel like grabbing him and gagging him when he swears at you; you will feel apprehensive to say the least when you hear the furniture flying around, and you will be almost uncontrollable by the time he rushes down into the kitchen. When he finally swears at you, and you have the carving knife in your hand . . .

Clearly, in such a situation it is very difficult to remain detached, but if you are to deal effectively with your child it is vital that you do not become embroiled in his behaviour: if you let yourself go you may do him serious harm.

During such an episode you should focus on listening to what is happening. Do not respond with a counterattack by shouting and swearing back at him. Listen carefully to everything that he is doing and saying. He is venting his spleen on the world and you in particular. Think of him as reacting to the restrictions of school: he has been released from this and you are bearing the brunt of his frustration and anxiety.

Explain, demonstrate, rehearse and reward
Choose one single aspect of his inappropriate behaviour. For example, you may choose the fact that he threw his coat on the floor when he came in. Work on this part of the entrance scene only.

After the episode, when he has calmed down, talk to him in private. Explain, demonstrate and rehearse how he should hang his coat in the hall when he comes in. Do not be harsh or condemnatory when you do this. You are simply making sure that he knows exactly what you require.

The following day you could have a snack ready for him. If he comes in and hangs up his coat properly, you could give it to him. Do not say why he has got this small treat. If he does not hang up the coat, go through the process again. Repeat three times, each time having the goodies available for him if he does as you wish on the following day.

When he has got into the habit of doing this, or if your efforts fail, you could start to concentrate on another aspect of unwanted behaviour in the grand entrance scene. It is important to remember that the child with ADHD may be totally unaware of what constitutes appropriate behaviour: whenever he is behaving inappropriately you should recognise the need to explain, demonstrate and rehearse; whenever he is behaving well you should make a conscious effort subtly to reinforce this with a reward.

HELP HIM TO COPE

Help him to make friends

A child with ADHD will find it difficult to make friends: because of his unpredictable responses other children may tend to be wary of him; because of his inability to stay on task they may find him difficult to play with.

You can help him to gain friends. Most friendships develop through shared interests and activities, so if you have arranged for him to attend local clubs or societies and have been willing to accompany him in the initial stages, he may begin to make relationships. When you are choosing an organisation for him to attend, make sure that it is highly structured and that it has a strong focus of interest on something other than making friends. If your child can become enthusiastic about the activities of the organisation, he will find that friendships begin to develop; if you emphasise that he is attending in order to make friends the opposite will occur. You could invite a number of his peers to your home to play with him. An advantage of this is that you can plan beforehand to ensure that this will be a success. Here are some guidelines:

a   Invite either one child or three
If you invite two there will be a likelihood of the two playing together and excluding your child; if you invite more than three the number may be too many for him to manage. If there are two or four children, including your own, you can plan paired activities.

b   Keep the sessions short
Make sure that everyone knows the time limit which you have placed on the session. Keep the sessions short rather than long.

c   Make contingency plans
It would be a good idea to prepare a number of activities which you can use when it looks as though difficulties are beginning to arise; rather than terminate a session you should deflect the children into another activity. The length of the session can then be modified for the next time.

d Supervise

Always be available to gauge how much you need to supervise the session; an older child may resent your presence, but at the time of a dispute you may subtly prevent problems escalating by asking him to help you with something or other. Keep at a distance and occupy yourself with some task. If he takes his friends into his room, keep checking on their activities by making excuses to enter: look for that odd dirty sock, or ask if he has a pen that you could borrow.

A younger child will always need you to be there: your role is to prevent him letting himself down. You should not wait for a crisis to occur before you intervene: try your hardest to anticipate any looming difficulties and use your imagination to deflect your child away from the centre of the problem.

Provide alternative activities

You should make sure that your child always has some kind of alternative activity to turn to—something which can prevent him letting himself down in front of his friends. As he gets older you will be able to discuss how, when he begins to become agitated, he can ensure that he has other things to do. Together you should make a list of appropriate activities which appeal to him. With a younger child you will need to have a simple list of contingencies which you can suggest to him whenever you feel that by doing so you will be preventing another episode of failure. When it is clear that things are going wrong you can suggest a temporary intervention with something from your list (see below); if you find that one of these alternative activities appeals more than others, use it regularly. You may find that after a while your child begins to use it himself as an automatic coping mechanism.

Provide structure

The activities you design can have another purpose: if you use them not just as emergency measures but as part of a regular schedule, they will provide your child with the structure he needs. We have discussed how very important it is for your child to belong to a social group outside your home: not only will he benefit, but you too will find the periods of respite a great help. Attending a group on a weekly basis can form part of this structure.

The child with ADHD will benefit enormously if he has a regular pattern to his life. Once he has fallen into the schedule it can provide him with a feeling of purpose and security. It can be the perfect antidote to his tendency to be easily distracted and impulsive. A list of activities could be devised around some basic elements:

a *Personal responsibilities*
1   Washing the family car.
2   Taking the dog for a walk.
3   Maintaining part of the garden.

b *Personal discipline*
1   Going for a jog.
2   Music practice.
3   Cleaning his shoes.

c *Duty to others*
1   Shopping for an elderly neighbour.
2   Sweeping communal pathways.
3   Tidying the garage.

I realise that you may raise your hands in horror at the thought of your child performing any of these tasks: the potential for damage to both property and people could be enormous! Whatever you plan, you must always be prepared to join him on at least the first occasion in order to estimate how realistic the activity is. You must make sure that there is every chance that he is going to be able to perform it well: if he can it will become an attractive alternative activity for him to turn to when he begins to feel out of control.

If it is clear that your child is unable to use any of your alternative activities, simply adjust them or think of others which centre around the three elements mentioned above.

Provide practical solutions
You cannot cure your child's condition; rather, you have to concentrate on providing the scenario which is least likely to promote the undesirable appearance of secondary behaviours. As he de-

velops he himself will adopt subtle coping techniques to avoid failure and embarrassment, but there are some initiatives which you could take.

Define procedures

According to the age of your child, and if it is appropriate, discuss those times of the day which seem to cause difficulties for him. Make a list of them in order of priority. Select the first one on the list and break down the task into simple stages.

For example, if he becomes confused and disorganised in the bathroom each morning, you should discuss everything with him and make a list of what he has to do in the order that he must do it. With a young child you should use symbols rather than words. Highlight the symbols or words with colours: he may find it easier to remember the colour sequence. Rehearse the sequence with him, referring to the list, until you feel sure that he understands what it says.

Encourage him whenever possible to refer to the list, and reward him when he begins to get the routine correct.

Clarify plans

You can avoid many problems by sitting down with your child at the beginning of each day and making a note of the things which you intend to do. If, as you make notes, you talk through the day with the young child, you will be communicating with him: he will know what the plans are and will not behave badly through frustration.

You will also, however, be introducing him to the idea of keeping a notepad, which could be an invaluable help to him as an organiser and an aide memoire. Later he may find it useful to invest in an electronic personal organiser.

List priorities

As you introduce him to the idea of keeping a notepad you should stress the process of making priorities. If he wants to do a number of things and is undecided which he might do first, you should encourage him to place them in a numbered order of preference.

1   Take dog for walk.
2   Play with computer.
3   Watch television.

Consider pros and cons
If your child finds it impossible to decide on something, you should encourage him to make a list of the reasons for and against each course of action.

For example, if he is frustrated because he cannot decide whether to watch television or take the dog for a walk, you should help him to write down the following:

	Reasons for	Reasons against
Taking the dog for a walk: 1		
2		
3		
Watching television: 1		
2		
3		

These are very simple processes but it is necessary to explain them. In doing so you will be introducing your child to techniques whereby he can focus his thoughts. His condition may be such that he will find this kind of tool very helpful. Later in life he may be able to dispense with the written forms and adopt the techniques as conscious thought processes.

Keep a diary
As the day ends you should spend a moment or two making notes in a diary. The diary could centre around the following:
    a   People.
    b   Places.
    c   Activities.
    d   Food.
    e   Feelings.
With the younger child you should begin by talking about your day; later he will talk to you about his. You should then let him watch as you enter your thoughts into a diary. When he is old enough you should provide him with his own and help him to make

entries. Later he will be able to do this privately and independently.

Keeping a diary can not only provide your child with another regular activity: it can help him to crystallise his thoughts and pull himself together. If you can encourage this routine in childhood, then for the rest of his life he will have a mechanism whereby he may assess his personal position, 'unload' his problems, sleep easy at night and feel strengthened for the next day.

At the very least he will be able to refer to the diary when he is unsure whether or when something happened; it could provide him with a greater sense of sequence, and in a practical way make his life much more ordered.

Help with homework

Having regular homework assignments, no matter how small, can be of enormous benefit to the child with ADHD, providing there has been adequate planning beforehand. If homework is regularly assigned it will provide another anchor point for him. You can help your child to achieve the maximum benefit from his homework periods by considering the following guidelines:

PRE-SCHOOL
1 Introduce him to the idea of a regular, special time during the day when he sits with you and looks at books/draws/paints, etc.
2 Explain the target at the beginning of these sessions—for example, to read from here to there.
3 Praise him when he achieves the target.

SCHOOL AGE
1 Continue with the 'homework' sessions whether or not he receives any from his school.
2 Make sure that your assignment is broken up, with rest periods if necessary, into sections small enough for him to complete each successfully.
3 When his work load becomes unwieldy, help him to create a schedule based on priorities.
4 Encourage him to set targets for himself.
5 Accept that your child may require different working conditions from yourself: he may be able to do his homework

better when he is listening to music, rather than having to focus on it in silence.

6   Consider the possibility of hiring someone to coach him during his homework periods.

In general you should try to see the homework periods as an effective therapeutic tool for your child: make them enjoyable, special times from the beginning, and do not use them to discipline him in a punitive sense.

If you find yourself doing this it may be because you are tired of having to supervise your child. Providing him with a tutor would be a way of avoiding this; it would also be a way of introducing another significant person into his life. But do make sure that the tutor understands the underlying purpose of the homework period, that he regards himself as someone who is there to share and encourage, that your child likes him and that he is able to think of himself as a coach rather than a teacher.

At all costs you should make sure that the homework periods do not become an effective weapon for your child to use against you. To avoid this you must do all you can from an early age to make them a pleasurable experience: if they provide him with a period of respite rather than another pressure point, he will impose them on himself.

If your child continues to experience difficulties with his homework you should consult his school and jointly devise strategies (Chapter 10) whereby an effective reinforcement programme can be implemented.

HELP HIM TO SETTLE

A child with ADHD may over-focus on something: he can become obsessional about such things as computer games or football. At these times he will stay on task and appear settled. However, his ability to sustain concentration across a range of interests is limited. Usually he is easily distracted and does whatever his impulse fancies. Because of his unpredictability his very presence makes others restless.

As he grows older it is important for you to discuss his difficulties and try to help him manage his condition: if he has no way of dealing with it, he will make more enemies than friends and in his isolation will develop a multitude of personal problems.

From an early age you can introduce him to techniques which, with maturity, he will develop to suit his needs. We have already discussed some examples and here are three others which should be built into his repertoire as soon as possible. We would all benefit by adopting these coping strategies; a child with ADHD would find them invaluable.

1 Relaxation

a   Choose a time when you are on your own with your child. Make the time slot a regular part of his daily schedule. Choose a place where it is peaceful and calm.

b   If he is young, use your imagination and turn the exercise into a game; if he is older simply tell him what you would like him to do.

c   Work with him until you feel confident that he is capable of practising on his own.

d   If you think it appropriate, have some relaxing background music.

EXERCISE ONE

Ask him to sit in a chair and to assume a comfortable position. Then say the following:

Close your eyes and take some deep breaths in time with me . . .
Breathe in quietly, slowly and deeply . . . and now slowly breathe out.
Breathe in again . . . and slowly breathe out . . .
In again . . . and out . . .
Listen to the sounds around you . . . find a sound outside . . .
Listen again to the sounds around you . . . find a sound inside this room . . .
Breathe in again, slowly . . . and breathe out . . .
Breathe in again, slowly and deeply . . . and breathe out . . .
Count slowly to yourself, with me, and as you count see the numbers in your mind . . .
One . . . two . . . three . . . hold number three in your mind . . .
make it bigger . . . and now see if you can give it a colour . . .

Count on . . . four . . . five . . . six . . . hold six, and see six bells
. . . hold them in your mind . . . and count on . . .
Seven . . . eight . . . nine . . . ten . . .
Breathe in . . . and slowly breathe out . . .
Breathe in . . . and slowly breathe out . . .
Slowly count to yourself from ten to one . . . with me . . . ten . . .
nine . . . eight . . . . . . one.
Now slowly open your eyes.

When your child has been introduced to this kind of regular,
time-specific relaxation exercise you should encourage him to use
the technique at other times during the day when he is feeling
under pressure. The above exercise could be adapted for this
purpose: he could keep his eyes open, focus on breathing slowly
and deeply, and quietly count up to ten.

The psychology of this age-old technique is that having something to do when things go wrong gives you a sense of control—
and usually helps to avoid the promotion of other problems.

2 Focusing

Focusing is not simply about concentrating on the here and now:
it is about getting to know yourself, being in touch with your
feelings and ultimately assuming a greater degree of self-control.

Relaxing and focusing complement each other: begin by getting
your child to relax himself and then provide him with exercises
which might help him to develop his capacity not simply to focus
but to feel. When he is relaxed, ask him to close his eyes and
perform the following exercise:

EXERCISE TWO

1   SEE and hold the following images in his mind for ten seconds:
    a   A mirror with his own face in it.
    b   His own name drawn on smooth wet sands.
    c   A red circle on a black square.

2   FEEL, and hold in his mind, for ten seconds, the sensation of
    touching the following:
    a   A balloon.
    b   A cat.
    c   A rope.

3   TASTE the following and hold the sensation in his mind for
     ten seconds:
     a   Ice cream.
     b   Lemonade.
     c   Toothpaste.

4   SMELL the following and hold the sensation in his mind for
     ten seconds:
     a   Fried bacon.
     b   Freshly cut grass.
     c   Cooked cabbage.

5   HEAR the following and hold the sound in his mind for ten
     seconds:
     a   A police car.
     b   A cuckoo.
     c   A kettle boiling.

You should adjust the list to suit your child: he will be frustrated
if you choose items which are beyond his experience. Also,
although you should gradually increase the length of time he is
asked to focus on the items, your primary objective should be to
enhance the quality of his feelings.

Try the exercises yourself beforehand. If you find them enjoyable and worthwhile, go through them with him. Your personal
enthusiasm for anything you want him to do is an essential requirement for success.

You could devise your own series of relaxation and focusing
exercises based on the above principles.

3   Physical exercise

We have already discussed, in Chapter 7, the benefits of disciplined physical exercise to the child with ADHD. You should
introduce your child to pleasurable physical exercises at an early
age; as he grows older, regular physical exercise should become
a normal part of his daily routine.

General guidelines

NEVER

a   Force your child to take part in team games.
b   Deride his physical ineptitude.
c   Project that for him to be a 'success' he has to have sporting ability.

ALWAYS

a   Focus on your child's personal fitness.
b   Carefully assess his abilities.
c   Select activities for their capacity to promote:
   1   a sense of achievement
   2   sustained interest
   3   support from others

Exercises

If you focus on your child's personal fitness he will become more confident, and when he is ready he will take part in group activities.

To achieve personal confidence you should provide him with a schedule of exercises that he can perform privately on a daily basis. He should be given achievement targets that are just beyond his reach, but which he will be able to achieve within an allotted period of time. His full exercise schedule should be made up of three elements:

a   Repetition exercises, with clearly defined targets.
b   Running or swimming, with clearly defined targets.
c   Recreational game, such as squash or table tennis, with yourself or another informed adult.

As with other recommendations, it will be important for either you, or an enthusiastic 'coach', to take part, at least initially. If you do not, you will be unable to estimate the suitability of the programme and your child's enthusiasm will quickly disappear.

Group activities

When you think he is ready, you should arrange for your child to take part in group activities, so that he can reap the benefits of regular scheduled meetings with people other than his family.

As I mentioned earlier, the child with ADHD often has a capacity for over-focusing, for becoming obsessed with something. If you can introduce him to regular physical exercise and recreational sport, he may use this capacity to a positive end: he may become a very good sportsman or, as a committed member of a club, he may develop a network of supportive relationships. At the very least he will be physically fit, and as a consequence he will feel good about himself and more able to control his impulses.

Martial arts
You should seriously consider encouraging your child to join a martial arts club. A central aim of such associations is to develop a person's self-control through disciplined physical routines. Some focus more on this aspect than others: T'ai Chi Chuan, for example, could be extremely useful as a discipline which will promote both physical fitness and personal congruence.

Church
Even if you yourself are an unbeliever, you should recognise that religion could offer your child a great deal. Daily prayer may serve the purpose of focusing him on someone outside himself and be a source of strength; it may provide him with another opportunity to crystallise his thoughts and feelings at the end of each day. Attending church on a Sunday may be a trial to begin with, but could prove to be a lifeline for him in the future: it could provide him with a genuine network of support.

CONCLUSION

This book was written because so many parents struggle on with their child. Driven to distraction by his difficult behaviour, they feel guilty, helpless and out of control. If you have a child who has behavioural problems you must seek help: if you do nothing he may ultimately become a delinquent, alienated from society and a threat to everyone. Teachers, doctors, members of the family, friends, neighbours and priests can become a helpful network of support if you involve them. Ask yourself how many of these you have spoken to, or whether you have preferred to keep your worries and concerns to yourself. Because of shame, have you sacrificed your child's interests for your own?

There *are* things you can do to help your child. In this chapter we have looked at ways of creating a home life that might make it easier for you and your child to cope with his condition; we have looked at some techniques that you may initiate and which he can develop and carry on into adulthood. The measures suggested are useful for us all to use, but they are essential survival tools for the child who is distractible, hyperactive and at the mercy of his impulses.

9   What Can be Done at School?

As a teacher, the first thing you should do is to acknowledge the theory of natural variation. When you enter your classroom you should accept that in all respects each pupil is different from the next. Each exists at a different point on a distribution curve in terms of intelligence, physical build, co-ordination, temperament and so on. You should not picture pupils as all being the same, sitting together on a plateau: if you do, you will experience frustration and failure. Whenever one appears to fall off the plateau you will regard him or her as a nuisance. You will be in no frame of mind to cope with any pupil who is brighter or more resilient than the rest; you will regard him as an aberration who is in the way of progress.

You definitely will not be able to cope with a child who may have ADHD.

If you accept that we all exist on a curve, with no two people occupying the same position, and that our places on the curve may change not only according to our various attributes, but in relation to the circumstances around us, then you may be able to begin by accepting each and every child for what she is.

You may say that this is fine in theory, but that when you have a class of twenty or thirty your only course of action is to exclude a child who does not conform.

A child with ADHD can present you with such terrible difficulties that you may be tempted simply to reject him or her in this way. Even in a class as small as eight she may prove unmanageable. However, you should not reject her or exclude her: you should assess her condition and make sure that she is placed in the right setting. You should acknowledge that her behaviour is a symptom of her condition—her particular position on the curve. No child should ever be excluded: if she is, it is an indication that the Code of Practice (Appendix B) has not been followed as early as it should have been.

Just as important as accepting the theory of natural variation is your acknowledgement that the child who is causing you so many problems has more than a few herself. Because of an innate condition she is impulsive, hyperactive and distractible. She cannot help this: she is relying on you to design a setting which will help her to cope.

You may find it useful to think of her as a handicapped child: you are not going to be able to cure her condition, but you can adjust things so that her quality of life improves dramatically. Another thing to bear in mind is this: as a child with ADHD grows towards adulthood she learns to adapt to her condition. Your role is to minimise the development of secondary, undesirable behaviour patterns as she goes through childhood. There are many adults who have ADHD and who have consciously and unconsciously devised personal coping techniques. If you can help this child to go through her school years without the development of other complications you will have achieved a great deal.

Finally, you should check the way in which you regard the parents of your pupils. Teachers usually condemn parents when their children misbehave: they attribute poor behaviour to weak parenting skills. This approach is understandable when a child has the ability to control his or her behaviour, but if she is distractible, impulsive and hyperactive at birth, such an attitude is prejudiced, unproductive and unprofessional. Again it may be useful to consider the very difficult child as handicapped: she is at the mercy of her impulses. Just as you may make special provision for a child with epilepsy and adopt an understanding approach to his parents, so you should consider it your responsibility to make similar adjustments to meet the needs of the child with ADHD.

When you adjust the classroom for a child who has this condition you should try to create an environment which will cater for her distractibility, impulsivity and hyperactivity. This may involve considering the nature of the furnishings and layout of the classroom. It may also involve examining the chemistry of the group of children or adults with whom she is supposed to interact; it may mean taking a very careful look at the activities that make up her school day.

PHYSICAL SAFETY

Your first consideration should be the physical safety of all children in your care: when you are aware that you have a child who is particularly impulsive you must take all the measures you can to guarantee both her safety and the safety of those around her.

A child with ADHD will not only have a high degree of impulsivity, she will be excessively sensitive and may react with impulsive, angry outbursts. When she is upset she may seize the first object to hand and use it to attack someone or even to self-mutilate. She may suddenly run around the classroom, and in an uncontrolled way smash into the corners of desks and injure either herself or others. In practical lessons such as Science, Physical Education or Craft Design and Technology she will present an even greater risk.

Although it will not be possible for you to cover all eventualities, it is extremely important for you to make an accurate assessment of potential problems and to take all necessary and reasonable measures to provide the safest possible environment. Dangerous objects such as scissors should be locked away; when they are needed you should be very conscious of the need to monitor their use; when you design the layout of your classroom and a child's place in it, you should try to minimise the possibility of her harming herself when she needs to 'escape' from a situation (see A Private Space, p. 154). The services of a classroom assistant are invaluable in achieving this very basic but essential objective (see p. 159).

Never hesitate to express your concerns to the headteacher if you are unhappy with the level of care you are able to provide. Admitting your inability to cope with a difficult child is the first step towards achieving some kind of positive resolution; not to do so could be classed as negligence, if a child came to serious harm while in your care. Use the procedures which I suggest in Assessing and Planning (p. 166).

HELPING THE CHILD TO COPE

Alternative activities

When you are preparing your classroom you should design it in such a way that there is a multitude of things to do. So many classrooms, especially at the secondary level, have nothing but chairs and desks in them and promote difficult behaviour rather than prevent it. All children would benefit if their classroom contained material and equipment which could be used either as incentives for performance, or attractive alternatives to solid sessions of 'work'. The child with ADHD finds it extremely difficult to stay on task for lengthy periods of time and if alternative activities are not provided he or she will become extremely disruptive.

You should of course attempt to set her tasks which are within her reach: you can then reward her with an alternative activity. Moreover, if at any time she is having difficulty in coping with her work or with others, it will be possible to turn her towards something else: you may in this way prevent her from letting herself down with unsociable behaviour. You should not expect the child with ADHD to stay on task: rather you should prepare for the fact that she will not.

Most classrooms for younger children are equipped in this way, but the alternative activities are used solely as rewards for those who have performed well; to cope with the difficult child you may need to use them to prevent her from suffering because of her condition. The longer she can go without failing the greater the chance of her growing in self-esteem: the better she thinks of herself the less defensive she will become, and the more able to control her impulses.

A private space

The child with ADHD may find it difficult to cope with other children, and because of her unpredictability she can be a threat to them. Also, because she is easily distracted, trying to stay on task with others around may be impossible for her.

The classroom arrangements should cater for these characteristics. Although the effect of external stimuli on children with ADHD is uncertain, the difficulty such children have in coping with others cannot be doubted.

If possible there should be private spaces where children can have their own belongings and to which they can retreat when the need arises. In the usual, larger classes, desk space is the nearest one can achieve to this, but private study booths can easily be constructed from cardboard refrigerator packaging, and with desks inside can be situated in corners or against walls to provide a realistic and cheap alternative. If at least three are provided, they will be there for all children to use. The child with ADHD will find them invaluable: she may even begin to self-regulate her behaviour by going to them as the need arises. She might take her work to an empty booth to complete it, or may find appropriate work permanently there for her. If a computer with suitable graded programmes is there and if she has been shown how to access her level, it will become a respectable alternative activity for her; a tape recorder and headphones could provide a similar opportunity. The booths should be promoted as an attraction for all pupils, and should never be used as punishment.

The group setting

Making changes
You should not expect the child with ADHD to get on with others: the fact is that she has difficulty in this, and you should recognise the characteristic as a handicap. When she is strong enough in herself she may feel able to integrate, but you cannot force her to do so without promoting disruptive behaviour. Make sure therefore that there are facilities for her to work on her own.

When you first receive her into the classroom setting you should arrange the class so that the chemistry stands a chance of success. Careful study of the personalities in your group may make it possible for you to see where the child with ADHD could be placed to minimise the chance of difficulties arising. Often a child may react badly with another one, and simply by rearranging the seating the problem is solved.

By altering the subgroups in the class you may find that the difficult child will become less so. It is in the interests of all the children for their groups to be changed from time to time, but for the child who finds it hard to relate to others it can be an extremely useful opportunity for a fresh start. If you do rearrange the groups, do not single her out; if the whole class is not to be changed around, then move at least three other children.

If the child with ADHD is working well in her group it is better that any changes should be minimal. She will prefer it if no changes are ever made, so it will be up to you to look at the chemistry of the group setting and make objective decisions as to how it can best operate. Always be on the lookout for ways in which you can alter the setting in order to improve the chances of her remaining calm; never assume that you have to put up with the status quo. You could ask yourself whether it is you rather than the child who cannot take the risk that is incurred with change.

When you are placing the child with ADHD in the classroom, remember that you are trying to provide her with the safest possible physical and psychological setting. She may feel safer if you place her in a corner; she may feel more secure if her desk is next to yours.

Cultivating group support

Whatever measures you take, it is likely that the behaviour of the child with ADHD will make her stand out from the remainder of the group: they will know that she is different. You can minimise the negative effect of this by continually stressing that none of us is the same: while we all have similar basic requirements, we also have unique special needs. You can also stress that we are not here to beat each other in either academic or practical work, but to help each other fulfil our maximum potential.

These are well-established principles in good special schools. Children are taught to appreciate that because each has his own needs, each may be treated differently. In this way children might come to recognise that people are individuals and begin to respect them as such. The stigma attached to disablement might begin to disappear. The themes should thread through your general approach, and as children become older you can be more explicit and direct.

If you have cultivated an atmosphere of positive, mutual support, the negative effects of any child behaving inappropriately will be minimised. The other children will find it easier to accept the child with ADHD; they may begin to regard her behaviour as separate and something which has to be treated. Instead of rejecting her they may support her. When she behaves badly they may be able to resist reacting to her behaviour; they may even be able to extinguish her behaviour by ignoring it. If you covertly encourage them to pay attention to her when she is behaving well, this may be even more effective.

None of this will be possible if you have been unable to foster a strong sense of belonging with the whole group. To do this you will need to organise outings and events which are over and above your usual timetable obligations. This may be a rather onerous commitment, but unless you take it you will be losing an excellent opportunity to cope very effectively with the behaviour of your group. Time spent with them in the world outside reaps great rewards and will be reflected in the response you receive from them when you require their support.

When extracurricular group activities are planned you should pay special attention to the needs of the child with ADHD. You should avoid excluding her from these because of her behaviour: you will be worsening her condition if you make her feel rejected. Instead, volunteer adults should be recruited to look after the needs of all children on a general basis: they may then focus on helping children who have difficulty in coping. If you plan beforehand, and discuss with your helpers what might be done to make it possible for this very difficult child to take part, you can with a little imagination turn an onerous task into a worthwhile challenge.

Paired responsibilities
The child with ADHD has usually developed low self-esteem, and any opportunity there may be to enhance this should be taken. If it is possible for her to assume certain duties and responsibilities, let her have them. Do not resent giving her these positions; if you are in the frame of mind where you can say that she does not deserve them, you have regressed into the position in which you possibly found yourself when you began to read this book—full of negative thoughts. As a disabled child she needs these crutches; so long as you are looking at her needs objectively it is possible to accord her privileges and status without appearing to reward her unacceptable behaviour.

Perhaps your main fear is the reaction of others in the group, but if you have cultivated an appreciation of individual needs this will be unfounded. Whenever possible you should pair the difficult child with another capable and more stable pupil.

Often a child will respond well to this arrangement: the responsibilities can be shared, success may be more likely, and there might even be the possibility of a friendship. Not only may the child with ADHD benefit from having a useful role model, but the other pupil will have his skill in dealing with others put to the test.

Appropriate work

All children should start with work which they can do, and progress from there. If they experience initial success they will be confident enough to tackle new material. The child with ADHD may have huge gaps in her learning and if you are not aware of these you may give her work which will aggravate her condition.

It is vital, therefore, that you can make an early assessment of her capabilities. If you are unable to do this yourself, consult your headteacher and ask for advice. Following an assessment you should make an Individual Education Plan in which precise details of how you plan to meet her needs are recorded (see p. 168). Central to your thinking should be an acknowledgement that the child with ADHD finds it difficult to stay on task, so the work she is given should be broken up into small stages which can successfully be completed within her attention span. You should also know what she is going to do as an alternative between each stage.

If a child with ADHD is given work which she can successfully complete, she will feel good about herself and will want to do more—the process is self-reinforcing. You should therefore focus on success rather than on dragging her through the curriculum. If you worry about this you will not only aggravate her condition but drive yourself to distraction.

If progress is to be made it will come only from an understanding that you are dealing with a child who is handicapped: if you think otherwise—that she is quite capable but is simply being awkward or deliberately naughty—you will be heading for disaster.

THE NEED FOR RECRUITS

If you are to implement any of the suggestions which I have made so far you will need help. Whether you are attempting to deal with the child with ADHD in a large group or a small one, you will not succeed on your own; no matter what you do for him or her there will be times when you will feel ready to snap, and unless you have someone there to give you either practical help or moral support you may find yourself in a dangerous situation.

Never struggle on, feeling that you are expected to cope and that to ask for assistance is to admit failure. A child with ADHD can be extremely demanding and may take you to the point where you lose control. You may find yourself accused of negligence should matters escalate into physical violence; in the absence of another adult you may even lay yourself open to charges of abuse.

Colleagues

You should always be very frank with your colleagues about children who cause you concern; you will find that they, too, often have difficulties with the same child and will be keen to reciprocate support.

You should explain that you are trying to cope with this difficult child and try to devise strategies to prevent him from letting himself down in front of the other children. For example, if you felt that he was becoming restless, you could send him to your colleague on a coded errand, or you could arrange beforehand that your colleague should be sent for and should come to your room for the simple purpose of creating a new focus of interest. Her sudden presence might be enough to seize the child's interest and deflate a potentially harmful situation.

Classroom assistants

If you have a very difficult child in your class you should ask your Education Authority to consider providing you with a classroom assistant. She could be effectively used to implement all the above suggestions: she could either focus on the child with ADHD or help the remainder of the class as you provide the child with special attention.

Having a classroom assistant would allow you to use your

imagination when it came to lessening the sense of frustration felt by the impulsive child. She could take the child out on an errand; she would have the time to focus in on him and see that he enjoyed progressively longer periods of time relating to other children in a positive way.

Classroom assistants, if trained and supervised, can be an extremely effective method of meeting the needs of the child with ADHD; they can help to avoid the situation where you feel that you must recommend that the child be removed from mainstream schooling.

Parents

Parents of children who are doing well at school make themselves known to teachers; but often the parents of a child who is experiencing difficulties will have little contact. You should take the initiative in this respect and invite the parents of such children to come to see you. Better still, you should arrange to go and meet them in their own home. Visiting a child's home can help to form a very useful bond between yourself, the child and his parents. If it is clear that they are against the idea do not press them, and when you meet them bear in mind that the purpose is to listen and understand, not to lecture or make judgements.

If you cultivate a good relationship with the parents of a child with ADHD, you will be doing wonders for him. In general terms, research indicates that if you support the parents you will be helping the child.

If the parents are hostile, be patient: they have agonised over themselves and their child for many years. You need to listen and support, not to add fuel to fire. When they want advice they will ask for it, and when you give it acknowledge that no one really knows the answers; one can only agree to experiment with different strategies. If you can support and recruit the parents you will find that they have great potential when it comes to effecting change in the child's behaviour.

You should, however, deter them from coming to help in the classroom. Difficult children will often react in a negative way when their parents are present: they are often unable to cope with those who are close to them, or in the presence of their parents may sustain the behaviour patterns encountered in the home. Although these behaviours are secondary to the condition of the child with ADHD, they are a complication which you can do without. If you invite the child's parents to school you should do so at a time when you can give them your undivided attention, and when their child might wait in the playground with your assistant. Parents of difficult children need a special time and place; they also need a special person such as yourself who can understand how they have been driven to despair by the child they love.

Friends and professionals

You should always bear in mind that difficult children have a great capacity to wear you down; you can easily get things out of perspective.

Find someone outside your immediate work situation to share your problems. You may find someone at home is close enough to understand but far enough from your work to see the wood from the trees. Do not presume that only a qualified person can help. Everyone has his own life skills, and you may find that a bit of homespun philosophy provides you with a way out of your impasse. You must of course keep all names and details which might identify a child out of your conversation, but otherwise let it all fall out; your friends will find the intensity of your work fascinating. If they provide you with no answers they will at least have shared your feelings and you should feel stronger because of this.

THE APPROACH

There are several techniques which may be used to address problems experienced by the child with ADHD. A token economy system might be devised or behavioural contracts mutually agreed; a child could be introduced to a system of recording which might help him to monitor his behaviour. Teachers will know of these techniques and others which can be employed to help a child adjust his behaviour.

Behavioural techniques work for the child with ADHD because he responds well to clearly defined targets and structured ways of achieving them. Self-monitoring techniques work because they make a child more aware of his behaviour; he is able to adjust his lifestyle and appears more in control.

In general terms, any strategies you devise should embody the following elements:

Structure

Clearly defined rules
Although you must cater for the short attention span of the child with ADHD by providing an attractive classroom setting with lots of alternative activities, this does not mean that you should simply allow the child to go from one activity to another, effectively doing what he wants.

At the beginning of each session you should set the goals and targets and tell him precisely what he will be doing. If you or your assistant sense that the predetermined plan is not working, that you have misjudged the suitability of the set task, then you must turn him to one of the alternative activities, but do not allow him to make this decision for himself. He needs someone else to be in control and operates best in a situation where rules and regulations are clearly defined. He is distractible, impulsive and hyperactive and you must provide him with the structure that he so desperately needs.

Clear communication between you and the child is extremely important. You must always explain your requirements to him in a patient and positive manner; you should face him with consequences of his actions, but do focus on rewarding his behaviour rather than punishing him (see Chapter 7).

Rules should be displayed in the classroom and the child should be referred to them, quietly but consistently and regularly, by you or your assistant.

Regular procedures
Classroom routines should be devised not only for practical reasons, but to enhance the structure which the classroom may provide for children who are disorganised within themselves.

Routines should be seen as an essential part of the overall behavioural programme which you are providing for your children and in particular for the child with ADHD. You should not adopt the attitude that children will only respond to rules and regulations that have a 'practical' purpose; all children need boundaries and parameters within which to work, and the younger they are the more they will be relying on you to provide them. Routines, rituals, traditions—whatever you may call them—are needed by the child with ADHD: they add to his feeling of belonging and provide a structure within which he may feel contained and secure. Here are some questions related to classroom routines for you to consider:

a   How do children enter the room?
b   How to they ask questions?
c   Who gives out the books and pencils?
d   What do they do when they have finished their work?
e   What happens at the end of a lesson?

Children should be very clear about what you have decided regarding these matters: you may need to demonstrate and rehearse them a number of times to the child with ADHD.

Organisation

The more organised you are in your approach to work, the more successful you will be. You will need to be highly organised to meet the needs of the child with ADHD, who can present you with such a multitude of unexpected problems.

If you feel that you have difficulty in organising yourself for this purpose you will appreciate how the child himself feels: because he is distractible, impulsive and hyperactive by nature he experiences gross difficulties when it comes to organising his life. You can help him to become more organised by:

a   establishing rules for neatness and tidiness—for example, making sure that he underlines headings to his work, places attractive covers on his books and uses dividers in his files; making sure that children know where to put books, and so on;
b   encouraging him to make lists of what he has to do—for example, daily duties, homework assignments, social commitments;
c   keeping a supply of materials and equipment available to cater for the possibility that he may arrive without them—and become disruptive;
d   intermittently rewarding him whenever he does neat work;

e presenting a visibly organised classroom where:
   rules are explained and displayed,
   daily routines are demonstrated and upheld,
   terms are punctuated with traditional events,
   sanctions are simple to explain and are effectively applied.

Stimulation

It is often the experience of those working with children who are distractible, impulsive and hyperactive that they appear to become more so when they are exposed to activities which might have been expected to release their energies and control their condition. If, for example, they think that the child with ADHD will be calmer after they have taken him to the swimming pool, they are invariably disappointed. He will appear even more at sea with himself. The assumption might be that the best place for him would be an environment where there was little or no stimulation.

However, this is open to question when one is attempting to deal with the distractibility of a child: it would appear to some experts that the child with ADHD will create his own distractions even if he is left in an environment with little else in it. Their theory is that underlying the poor attention span of a child with ADHD is a deficit in motivation. This is borne out by the way in which so many children with ADHD stay on task when they are given computer games or when they are receiving other similarly intense levels of stimulation.

The message would seem to be that if you want to combat the child's distractibility you will need to make sure that your classroom is full, rather than bereft, of stimulating activities. If you provide a controlled and regulated array of exciting things to do the child will have more opportunities to remain focused and on task; he will be less inclined to be impulsive and hyperactive and to become embroiled in unsatisfactory interactions with others.

The lack of structure, rather than the amount of stimulation, found in such activities as being in a swimming pool with others, promotes the problems of a child with ADHD.

Providing a rich and stimulating array of *controlled* classroom activities can also equip you with an effective hierarchy of rewards and a system of ensuring that the child with ADHD does not fail in front of others (see p. 154).

Self-help

Monitoring

An effective way of helping a child to cope with his or her behaviour is to encourage her to monitor it. You could, for example, discuss a particular aspect of her behaviour and tell her to keep a tally of the number of times it occurs; if she finds this too difficult you or your assistant could help her by devising a system which prompts her to add to the tally. For example, every time she talks out of turn you could touch her on the shoulder: this would be the signal for her to add to the tally.

Studies have shown that it is not really important whether or not the tally is correct: the very system itself can see a dramatic decrease in the frequency of unwanted behaviour.

Social skills

Another approach would be to focus on the child's inability to cope with others: she could be given a systematic programme of training in social skills. A specific situation could be selected and described in detail and the way in which she should manage this could be demonstrated and rehearsed. This is another useful way in which you could use your classroom assistant. Do not expect the child with ADHD automatically to know how to behave: she needs to be shown what to do and to practise in safety. Given a few basic instructions she may be able to cope on her own.

Counselling skills

To help the child with ADHD to gain positive reactions from others, you or your assistant could introduce her to some counselling skills. For example, you might demonstrate and rehearse through role play how to listen to a person's conversation, reflect on it and affirm it. The child who has ADHD is often unaware of the feelings and needs of others, and in this way, and others, you could try to help her to develop more meaningful relationships with them.

Finding solutions

A fourth approach might be to focus on the child's inability to cope with feelings of restlessness or indecision. She could be introduced to a set of simple rules which she might employ at these times. When she is feeling restless she might ask herself:

1 *Where* do I feel the restlessness?
2 *What* is causing me to feel this way?
3 *Who* should I tell about this?

When she is undecided about what to do she might ask herself:

1 *What* are my options?
2 *Which* is the one I want to take?
3 *Why* do I hesitate?

It will never be possible for you to cure a child with ADHD, but in these and other ways you will be able to help her cope with her condition. As we get older we all adopt skills which take into account our personal characteristics and compensate for any deficiencies. The child with ADHD needs help in this: if she does not receive it she is likely to become alienated and hostile to those around her.

ASSESSING AND PLANNING

The behaviour of a child with ADHD is distressing to those who meet him because it is so often diffuse and difficult to describe. One minute the child might be wandering about with no apparent purpose, the next he might be happily seated in the corner engrossed in a book; he may be angrily shouting at you or kindly asking if you want a cup of tea. He may be able to perform work adequately one moment and the next appear to have absorbed nothing. There is seemingly no consistency to his behaviour and because of this a person may feel uneasy in his presence and bewildered as to what to do about it. Distractibility, impulsivity and hyperactivity underlie his behaviour and make him unpredictable, unreliable and latently volatile. Dealing effectively with such difficult behaviour is a long-term project, and involves implementing the many suggestions I have made so far over the whole of a child's school career.

As with a marathon race, it may not be realistic for you to expect to win, but it is essential to make detailed plans if you want to complete the course and take the child with you. A sensible approach is to divide this long-term task into smaller stages and to set specific targets for each one. You must devise techniques and strategies to achieve your aims, regularly assess progress and make necessary adjustments: in the UK and elsewhere this principle is embodied in required Codes of Practice (Appendix B) which as a professional you are required to follow.

Assessing
Rather than defining your objectives in general terms, you should clarify precise behaviours which need to be addressed, and deal with these in order of priority.

New entries
As a classroom teacher you should be aware of a child's difficulties before he comes to you. Knowing the rough details of each child who is to enter your class can be enormously useful and can help you to plan for the child who is going to prove difficult from the start. A child with ADHD will not find it easy to enter new surroundings, and should you have prior warning of his arrival you can avoid immediate disaster. A poor entry can delay progress considerably. If details of new arrivals are not forthcoming, seek them out.

Incident sheet
When you observe a child exhibiting difficult behaviour and sense that he may have special needs, you should make a note of each episode. If you use an incident sheet (Appendix C) you may be able to adjust matters to alleviate the situation; later, when you need to refer the child to your headteacher and to follow the Code of Practice, you will find these detailed records enormously useful.

Maintain the incident sheets as a permanent feature of your system of recording; they will complement whatever type of assessment you have devised for the Individual Education Plan.

Planning

Individual Education Plan
Under the Code, expert help should be available to help you design an Individual Education Plan, but if there is a delay in achieving assistance or if you want to be effective from the beginning, you could use your incident sheets to formulate a preliminary one for yourself. Here is a possible layout:

Individual Education Plan

Name: Date of birth: Address:

Date of entry into present class:

General observations and aims:
    1   From previous records:

  and or 2   Present period of observation (dates):

Specific difficulties
  1
  2
  3
  4
  5
  6
  7
  8
  9
 10

Targeted difficulties in order of priority:
  1
  2
  3
  4

5
6
7
8
9
10

Target one:
Aim:
a Strategies to be employed:
    General: Staffing:
        Grouping:
        Equipment:
        Curriculum materials:
        Links with home:
        Involvement of external agencies:

    Specific: Techniques to be employed in school:
        1
        2
        3
        4
        5

b Method of assessment:
   How?
   By whom?
   Frequency?

c Length of time to be spent on this target:
  Date to be reassessed:

       Signed: Teacher..................Date: ....
            Assistant......................................
            Headteacher................................
            Parent...
            Co-ordinator ....
            External support ....

d Reassessment: Date:.........................
                          1 Was the Aim achieved? ....
            if so: 2 List the techniques in order of effec-
                             tiveness
                             ....
                             ....

            if not: 3 List five alternative techniques
                             ....
                             ....
                             ....
                             ....
                             ....

            and   4 Implement programme again (*tick or
                             delete*)
            or   5 Abandon Target number One and
                             begin on Target Two.
                             Signed: (as above)............. Date ....

CONCLUSION

The child with ADHD presents a complex problem for those who work or live with him; his behaviour can exhaust them because they simply do not know how to start to cope. To begin with, as a professional you should ensure that you have done all you can to guarantee the physical safety of the impulsive child and of those around him: this is your first responsibility. Only when you are happy that you are able to do this should you attempt to deal with him in the classroom setting.

You should then acknowledge that to do anything other than contain him you are going to need help; even to do just this will need another pair of hands. Your second requirement therefore is an assistant. If you can recruit an enthusiast who has an intuitive feel for difficult children and who can be trained to pre-empt problems, you will be able to implement the suggestions I have made in this chapter and elsewhere, and provide an effective programme for the child with ADHD.

The challenge of dealing with such a child is enormous, for each day you may be faced with unpredictable reactions: you may feel that you are living on a knife edge. However if you have thoroughly assessed the situation, altered the environment, adjusted groups, devised strategies and made short- and long-term plans, you will have done just about as much as you can to minimise the possibility of the child suffering because of his condition. With the support and confidence of the child's parents, the encouragement of your colleagues and the advice of external agencies, you will be offering the best available service.

Whether this is enough is of course another matter. The child may not respond to any of your strategies, and it is then that you must propose to your colleagues on the IEP Assessment Team that they consider alternative solutions beyond the scope of your expertise. If you wish the child to remain with you he may be able to do this with the help of medication; if you feel that this is unacceptable you may propose that he would be better placed in a small special school.

Do not hesitate to admit that you are unable to meet his needs. When parents and professionals fail to do this, the condition of the child with ADHD is exacerbated. Be frank about your concerns; share your thoughts with the child's parents and with your colleagues: if you are to achieve anything with the child who has ADHD you must recruit all the help you can and be open to any alternative strategies that may be suggested.

10 Towards Resolution

If you have absorbed the underlying principles in this book and implemented the practical measures that I have suggested, you may have seen a marked improvement in the behaviour of your child. From being distractible, impulsive and hyperactive he may have become calm, focused and controlled. You may have been able to achieve this over a period of time by:

a   Becoming stronger in yourself and more objective in the way you look at his behaviour.
b   Adjusting his home life to provide him with consistency and controls.
c   Adjusting his school life to cater for his specific learning difficulties and social needs.

The effect of these measures may have been considerably enhanced by a high degree of co-operation between the home and the school.

On the other hand, you may have been doing all of this for a considerable length of time and seen no improvement at all. Your child may seem to have got worse, and you may have become even more frustrated because of the special arrangements you have made and the many wasted hours you have spent trying to make a fresh start. No matter what you have done he may have continued to exhaust you with his unlimited energy, exasperate you with his lack of concentration, and frighten you with his unpredictable and impulsive behaviour.

If this is so, it may be that such is the severity of his condition that without the help of medication he will never settle and be in a position to benefit from everything that you and his school do for him.

A MULTIMODAL APPROACH

Just as a child who has asthma or epilepsy must have his condition controlled with medication before he can safely attend school or live at home, so too must the child with ADHD. The most effective approach, then, to dealing with your child's problem would be to determine as soon as possible whether he has ADHD and whether he would benefit from medication. Although I have provided guidelines, only a specialist can make these decisions.

If you are a parent and your difficult child is not yet attending school you should take him to see your doctor. If he is attending school, you should consult his teacher and discuss your concern that nothing you have done seems to make a difference. Talking to her may make you think that perhaps there are still some further strategies you both could try, but if not you should decide together whether it would be a good idea for you to visit your GP. If you are a teacher and have implemented the measures suggested in this book to no avail, you should not hesitate to mention to his parents and the Special Needs Co-ordinator that the child needs to be examined by a doctor.

For the very difficult child a multimodal approach is the only effective solution. Too often we read of individual cases in which medication alone has been administered, without an accurate analysis of the child's performance in the home and at school, leading to anguished complaints from parents whose bright and lively child has been given medication and turned into a docile 'vegetable'. To administer medication arbitrarily and without detailed reference to parents, teachers and other carers is clearly wrong and dangerous.

On the other hand we also know of many schools and parents who, because they do not acknowledge the distinction between those children who present difficult behaviour due to their life circumstances and those who do so as a result of having ADHD, aggravate the condition of the child by denying him medical treatment. When he finally becomes too much for them to handle their solution is to exclude him. Clearly this too is wrong.

Throughout this book we have examined what parents, teachers and paediatricians may offer. When each attempts to treat the child with ADHD in isolation there is a possibility that not only will the treatment prove ineffective, but it might even be harmful to the child. When they work in harmony they may provide a prescription potent enough to address the problems of most children with ADHD.

A CO-ORDINATED PROCEDURE

To make sure that everyone's efforts are co-ordinated it is essential that some kind of formal administrative structure is in place. This should be underpinned by a systematic programme of training.

Teacher training

If all teachers were trained to focus on children rather than their subject specialism a great many problems could be avoided. Training courses should embrace preventative techniques and give emphasis to the fact that teachers are employed because children need them as people. If the behaviour of children was seen as the primary concern of teachers rather than a secondary matter, then the delivery of the curriculum would proceed much more smoothly. Difficult children would not be seen as a nuisance; their needs would be met, and others would benefit as a result.

Teachers should be trained to recognise the symptoms of ADHD; they should learn how to deal with a child who presents these symptoms and what the procedures are for referring the child to others when they themselves are unable to meet his needs.

Special Educational Needs Co-ordinator

In each school in the UK there is a Special Educational Needs Co-ordinator. This person, if trained and accorded suitable salary and status, makes the ideal co-ordinator for the Multimodal Approach. Enormous sums of money, incurred by making special needs provision outside the mainstream setting, could be saved if the Special Educational Needs Co-ordinator were not only knowledgeable regarding Special Needs procedures, but had received special training in working with difficult children and families. He could then have the following responsibilities:

A   To co-ordinate procedures as outlined in the Code of Practice.
B   To develop and maintain an In-Service Training and support

programme for all teachers. Elements in this programme should include the following

a the management of difficult children in the classroom;
b whole school approaches;
c teaching styles;
d counselling skills;
e family matters.

C To develop links with schools and homes

a Liaise with feeder schools for the purpose of identifying potentially difficult children, forewarning their new teacher and advising her on suitable strategies.

b Encourage teachers to develop informal family support work.

Supporting families of difficult children can result in a dramatic decrease in the level of their disturbed behaviour. Parents are strengthened to the point where they can begin to control their children, while the children feel more secure and become less defensive. Each teacher should be encouraged to participate: if the Co-ordinator himself were to do all of the work he would be seen as a full-time social worker. Parents need to feel that they are working with someone who shares their problems rather than a trained professional who has statutory duties; the Special Educational Needs Co-ordinator should therefore continue to have his own subject specialism and teaching duties.

FINAL SOLUTIONS

Even when medication is administered and special adjustments are made in the home and school, some children with ADHD will not respond. Additional measures must then be taken, including the consideration of whether the child should remain in his present school, and whether he should continue to live at home.

Exclusion

The child may be excluded from school. If your child reaches the final stages of the exclusion procedure and is asked to leave, it is usually because it would not be in the interests of other children for him to remain there; he will have committed some serious offence. This may be a one-off episode, but because of its serious-ness it makes exclusion unavoidable. In most cases, however, the offence which results in exclusion is the last straw—the culmi-nation of a variety of antisocial episodes. By the time a child is excluded he will have become extremely unpopular and disliked by the remainder of the school.

It is therefore clear that it is not only in the interests of others but for his own benefit that he be removed and given the opportu-nity for a fresh start.

You should never fight against a proposal that your child be excluded from school: whether there is a sound reason or not (and usually there is), you can guarantee that if his exclusion has been suggested, he is not wanted there. You should realise that, despite what your child may claim, there is a very good chance of him lying to you about his behaviour. Children never like to disappoint their parents, and the more sensitive they are to their own failings the less likely they are to admit to their shortcomings. Your only cause for grievance might be that not enough has been done under the Code of Practice to help your child: a good indication of this will be the degree to which you have already been involved by the school in your child's affairs. If you have been consulted about his behaviour you will know how much has been done to help him.

Although the chance of this happening is becoming less, many children with ADHD have been excluded from school because their handicap has not been recognised. There are children under ten years of age who may already have been excluded from three or four schools. Their condition has been ignored by parents and professionals, their needs have gone unrecognised. If the number of exclusions is to be halted, special measures and procedures, such as those suggested in this book and included in the Code of Practice, must be adopted by all schools. In particular, if the notion were more readily accepted that difficult behaviour is a symptom of a hidden handicap, exclusion as a punitive measure might altogether cease to exist.

Ideally a child should never be excluded from a school. Instead, it should be recommended that, following the diagnosis of his condition and the extensive implementation of a multimodal treat-ment programme, it has been concluded that he is not well placed.

Each child should be placed in the setting which best meets his need—and without prejudice. This could happen if we were to embrace the theory of natural variation and if we were to use to good effect the structure that was invented to cope with it, namely our comprehensive system of education.

Looking at difficult behaviour and how to cope with it can, in this way, lead to positive outcomes rather than rejection and exclusion.

Personal tuition

If your child is excluded from school, or if it is felt that he would be better placed elsewhere, arrangements may be made for him to be taught at home by a visiting tutor until a new placement is found for him.

This may be a useful emergency procedure, but should only ever be temporary and for as short a time as possible. Receiving home tuition usually means that a tutor visits for a specified number of hours each week: the rest of the time the child is left on his own. Clearly his behaviour will only deteriorate further under these conditions, and when an alternative placement is found it will be more difficult for him to adjust to the idea.

Following exclusion your child may be sent to a tutorial unit, a small group setting where children are placed until a satisfactory permanent arrangement is in place. Again, everything must be done to ensure that the child's stay in the unit is short; the setting is a transitional one and in any other sense is of little benefit to him.

Day special schools

It may be suggested that your child would be better placed in a day special school, where the classes are small and the teachers are specially trained to deal with difficult children. These schools are particularly beneficial for those children whose families still feel that they can cope with them at home.

In these schools a difficult child no longer feels different from the rest. He is able to cope better with his condition and has a greater opportunity to demonstrate his abilities. He can become stronger in himself and feel less need to react defensively. Small, supportive groups, where there is a strong sense of belonging and purpose, and where it is possible for teachers not only to design Individual Education Plans but to implement them, can help a child with ADHD to cope not only when he is at school but when he is at home. Techniques can be suggested, rehearsed and put into practice on a daily basis.

Residential special schools

If you have made it clear that you can no longer cope with your child at home, it may be suggested that he be placed in a residential special school. These schools provide a degree of care and consistency that is beyond most parents: specially designed facilities are complemented by highly trained staff who, working shifts, provide a curriculum extending over twenty-four hours. They offer specialised help to the child and necessary respite to his parents. Some offer a small number of day placements or weekly boarding; others offer termly boarding or fifty-two-week provision.

Some residential schools are attached to hospitals. Here a child's behaviour is observed and recommendations made for treatment; medication may be administered and results monitored to achieve safe and effective dosage levels.

You should not feel apprehensive or ashamed at having to agree that your child would be better off in a residential school. As I have explained, many children find their greatest difficulty in the home setting. This is because they find it hard to cope with those close to them, and none is closer than a parent. You yourself probably find it easier to manage and control other children than you do your own. In an appropriate residential school your child may have less trouble relating to people and will benefit from the routines and consistency embodied in the educational and leisure programmes; you too will have time to become strong, to be able to cope when he visits.

Traditionally there are two approaches to dealing with difficult children in residence. Both see the improvement of self-esteem as a central aim.

a The accepting approach

This assumes that the child has suffered failure in the mainstream setting, that he has been unable to meet the requirements of the 'system'. He has suffered not only failure but rejection. He needs to be placed in an environment where he can feel complete acceptance; where he can begin to go through bonding processes missed during his formative years. A safe, warm environment is provided, with few demands made on the child and with a low level of expectation in terms of his behaviour and academic performance. The child grows and develops in this nurturing environment and is healed.

b The expecting approach

This assumes that for children to progress happily they must have rules and regulations in which to operate and a clear picture of expectations with regard to behaviour and academic performance. Exponents of this approach believe that if children know what they have to do to be good, then they can be so; they need to be provided with avenues of restitution. Regular routines and procedures can promote not only a sense of security but a sense of achievement, especially if they are consistently employed in a small, caring community.

You will need to consider which kind of approach would best suit your child. The child with ADHD usually responds best to a structured setting, but if you choose the expecting approach you will need to be reassured that the school acknowledges the innate condition of your child. It clearly would be wrong to place him in a school which believed that, given rules and regulations, he would be as capable of getting things right as the next child, and that sanctions would guarantee compliance.

You should seek reassurances that although the system is clearly a structured one, the ability of each child to conform to it is carefully assessed and that adequate measures are taken to help him experience success. You should also clarify the school's attitude to medication. Even schools which claim to specialise in dealing with difficult behaviour may be resistant to its use.

It is important that both you and your child are enthusiastic about the placement. If you are not it will soon break down. You may find that you have to be very strong and determined not to succumb to his homesickness during the first week or so, and if you are happy with the school in the first place this will help you enormously.

The right school for your child

When you are making these final considerations as to whether your child is actually well placed or whether there might be a better alternative, you should begin by asking yourself:

1   What is wrong with his present school?
2   Is there anything more that could be done for him at school?
3   What is wrong with his present home life?
4   Is there anything more that could be done to improve matters at home?
5   Is there an alternative kind of school that could meet his needs better?

To answer these questions fully you may have to reread this book! We have seen that there is a multitude of things for you to consider when you are trying to assess the behaviour of a difficult child and deciding what you might do about it.

These questions are suggested as a way of making a final check that you and your child's school have done all you can. Unless you have attempted to implement the strategies mentioned in Chapters 8 and 9, there will be little chance of your child attending the alternative school of your choice. Special education, and residential special education in particular, is expensive and will only be sponsored if you can give good evidence that all other avenues have been explored.

If you are unsure what schools can offer, you should make an appointment to visit them. Most schools are delighted to show prospective parents round, with no obligation. Here are some points to look for when you are trying to assess their suitability for your child:

1   *School*
a   Is the general atmosphere in the school happy and relaxed, or is there an air of tension and expectation of trouble?
b   Is the school approved for use under national regulations?
c   When was the school last inspected by the Department of Education/Social Services, and what were their conclusions?

2   *Philosophy and practice*
a   What is the central aim of the school?

b How does the school explain the behaviour of a child with ADHD?
c What part does medication play in treatment programmes?
d Is the headteacher friendly and approachable?

3 *Staff*
a Are all teachers qualified in working with children who have special needs?
b Are specialist subject teachers available?
c Are classroom assistants available?
d What is the pupil-teacher ratio?
e Are there men and women on the staff?
f Are care staff qualified?
g What is the pupil-child care staff ratio?
h Do the staff appear keen and enthusiastic?
i Are all staff vetted for working with children?
j Are specialist staff available for one-to-one work, for example for specific learning difficulties?

4 *Curriculum*
a Does the curriculum meet national requirements?
b Is personal support possible during lessons, and more especially during practical work?
c Is individual tuition in reading given?
d Do children take examinations?
e Is homework given and what special arrangements are made for the child with ADHD?
f Do trips and expeditions take place, and what measures would be taken to ensure that a child with ADHD could participate?
g Is leisure time structured and supervised?
h What are rising and bedtimes and what arrangements are made to supervise early risers and light sleepers?
i What arrangements are in place for parents to remain in contact with their children?

5 *Facilities*
a Are the children with their own age groups?
b Is contact between older and younger pupils minimal?
c Are showers and toilets and bedspaces designed for privacy?

d   Are dormitories attractive, and common rooms equipped with leisure facilities?
e   Is the dining-room clean and attractive?
f   Is the menu varied and nutritious?
g   Do children have a choice of food?
h   Are classrooms stimulating and attractive?
i   Do classrooms have facilities for private time?
j   Is there a wide range of facilities for sport and practical work?

6   *General*
a   Does it appear that the staff have a good level of control?
b   How is discipline upheld?
c   What are the arrangements for pastoral work?
d   Do you think that staff fully appreciate your child's condition and that you could entrust him to them?
e   Did you feel welcome?
f   Would you be proud for your child to attend?
g   If you were to describe the school to a friend, how would you sum it up?

When you have asked these questions, either during your visit or afterwards, you should try to picture your child in the school, and ask yourself whether, in relation to all these matters, he would benefit from being placed there. If you have responded positively to the questions, he will stand a good chance of being happy; if you have come up with a majority of negative replies, you should look elsewhere. As I mentioned earlier, your enthusiasm for the placement is essential if it is to succeed. Do not rush into matters: if you make the wrong decision your child will soon return home, feeling even more rejected than before.

PERSONAL RESOLUTION

Attention Deficit Hyperactivity Disorder is a biological condition that cannot be cured: it is present at birth and stays with a person throughout his life. As your child grows you can help him to learn to live with it until he is mature enough to make appropriate adjustments to his lifestyle.

The first and most important thing you must do is accept that his condition is biological. If you acknowledge this then your whole approach will fall into place: you will see your role as helping your handicapped child lead as full and meaningful a life as possible, rather than rejecting him as a deliberately naughty child or as an evil young adult.

You will see that there is a purpose to making special arrangements for him in your home or making adjustments in the school environment; you will see the value of considering medical treatment for him, and of co-operating with others to provide an effective multimodal approach. If you can help your child to survive into adulthood without developing antisocial tendencies or self-destructive introspection, you will discover that he is able to carry on from there using the skills you have taught him and developing effective strategies of his own. You will have guided him towards independence.

Let us make a final summary of the action you might take to achieve the maximum resolution for your child. We will break it down into simple stages:

Summary

1   Accept that some children are excessively distractible and impulsive, while others are in addition hyperactive. They are born this way, and special arrangements must be made to meet their needs. The child at the centre of your concern could have this condition which is described as Attention Deficit Disorder or Attention Deficit Hyperactivity Disorder.

2   As soon as possible have your difficult child examined: if he is below school age take him to your doctor; if he attends school consult his teacher.

3   Acknowledge that many children have behaviour problems which do not have a biological origin. A specialist will tell you if your child is one of these, or whether he has ADHD.

4   Accept that if your child does not have ADHD you will need to make
   a   adjustments in the home;
   b   adjustments at school.

5   Accept that if your child does meet the criteria for ADHD you will need to
   a   make adjustments at home;

b   make adjustments at school;
c   administer medication to him.

You will find detailed strategies elsewhere in this book.

A sixth stage is to consider how you may help your child in his adulthood.

ADHD in adulthood

As he grows up your child may need to develop techniques for combating any two or more of the following characteristics which are commonly found among those adults who are said by experts to suffer from ADHD:

1   emotional instability;
2   hot temper;
3   low tolerance of stress;
4   disorganisation;
5   impulsivity.

You should help him to do this by privately discussing his problems and together working out ways to manage them. Throughout his childhood you will have gradually introduced him to many detailed techniques related to these problems, but here are three more general suggestions which you may emphasise as he becomes older:

1   Membership of a group

Anyone who has a problem can gain enormous support by associating with others who have the same condition (see Appendix A for contact addresses). Urge him to join an association, to read as much as he can about his condition. Remind him that he is not the only one in the world who is disorganised or impulsive; there are many others who would appreciate it if he contacted them.

Joining any club would, however, do the trick: sharing an activity with others, and belonging to a group, can help to improve his self-esteem. When this happens he will become more in control of himself. If possible he should join a club which involves physical exercise. Exercising will make him feel good, and if it makes demands on him it can be both physically and emotionally strengthening.

Clubs which specialise in yoga or the martial arts would be a good option: their central aim is self-control and personal congruence. He should not hesitate to approach these enthusiasts: they have a sense of mission when it comes to new recruits.

2 Find a personal coach

If he can find someone who understands his condition, he or she will prove to be an invaluable source of strength to him, chivvying him along generally, and reminding him of his condition when he is becoming lost in it. This person will bully him into making lists and performing essential daily chores, calm him when he becomes overheated, and encourage him when his condition depresses him.

He should choose a friend or someone from outside of his immediate family: those closest to him may cause him more problems than they can solve. If he joins an association for sufferers of ADHD it might help another member if he or she were to help him, or vice versa: the best way to learn is to teach.

3 Accept yourself

Many adults who have ADHD spend their time denying that they have a problem. If your son is hot-tempered, impulsive, disorganised or excessively sensitive he should admit it. Neither he nor anyone else is to blame for his condition.

He should listen to what other trusted adults tell him about himself: accept what he is and stop pretending to be what he is not. He should not imagine that he is highly organised when his lifestyle is chaotic, and if in reality he has always relied on others to sort things out for him; he should not think that others regard him as calm and reliable when he knows in his heart of hearts that they have suffered because of his hot temper and impulsivity.

He should accept that ADHD is a biological condition, not a sign of a weak spot in his character: he has nothing to be ashamed of. He needs to face up to his inadequacies and take the measures I have suggested.

We must all accept that we are born with a unique personality: there is little that we can do about it other than accept it and learn to use it effectively and in the interests of others. When he has accepted himself for what he is, he will discover an enormous sense of relief: with some conscious adjustments and help from his association and coach he will be able to relax and live, rather than continually walking on a painful tightrope of self-doubt and uncertainty.

CONCLUSION

In Chapter 1 I told you the story of Liz Jones and her son Simon. Liz drove herself to the point of a nervous breakdown trying to cope with his behaviour.

If she and the teachers at her son's school had known about ADHD she could have avoided years of suffering, Simon would never have developed the foul language and antisocial behaviour that caused him to be excluded from two schools before he was nine years old, and his teachers could have been spared the daily humiliation he inflicted upon them.

When Dr Good spoke to Liz, his trained medical mind quickly analysed the possibilities. Having encountered many other such children, he recognised the severity of the problems which her son was presenting: he could have ADHD. If he were to focus on solving Simon's problems, the patient whom he had been called to see could be cured; if she were made well, she would be able to play a part in providing a permanent solution to the problem.

Within a day he had consulted a paediatrician who, through the school's Special Educational Needs Co-ordinator, arranged to interview and administer questionnaires to Mrs Jones and Simon's teachers. Thereafter at a meeting, called by the Co-ordinator, of all those concerned, the paediatrician announced his conclusion that Simon had ADHD. Together with the educational psychologist who had been invited, the group discussed possible adjustments that could be made in both the home and the classroom, and considered the recommendation that Simon receive medication.

It was agreed that the full treatment programme be implemented and that Simon's behaviour and performance both at home and at school be monitored on specially prepared forms. It was decided that after six weeks they should all meet to discuss his progress: however, if they were at all concerned beforehand they would not hesitate to contact each other.

As we saw in Chapter 1, after only one month it looked as though Liz Jones' problem was solved. She would have said that it happened sooner—that within half an hour of taking his medicine her son's behaviour had been transformed—but the success of the programme really began to dawn on her when she realised that he had been going to school for a full week without any reports of unacceptable behaviour, that she could not remember when she last said a cross word to him and that whenever she thought of him she pictured him, in her mind's eye, smiling and happy.

Concluding with this successful outcome would have been a happy way to end, but if other difficult children are to be understood and helped we must recognise that it was largely through misfortune and by chance that Simon Jones received treatment. Most parents feel that they are totally responsible for the behaviour of their child: like Liz Jones, they struggle on to the bitter end doing their very best to make him behave well. Most professionals expect all children to conform, and they reject a troublesome child; in desperation they blame the parents for his behaviour. Neither parents nor professionals find it easy to accept that the difficult behaviour of some children might be rooted in a biological condition.

If, however, they were to look at it in this way they could stop blaming each other and focus on providing the child with an effective, multimodal treatment programme.

If you are a parent, I hope that this book has helped you to understand the behaviour of your child. I hope that you can now accept him, despite the misery he causes you, as a separate human being who has to cope with severe personal problems: I hope that you will be even more determined to do everything you can to help him.

If you are a professional, I hope that you have become firmer in your resolve to focus on the personal needs of your children, and that you are now able to accept that there may be some among them whose severe behaviour difficulties reflect an innate biological condition. I hope that both parents and professionals can assume joint responsibility for such children, and that by openly expressing mutual support they can become stronger and more able to deal with the problems presented by the child with ADHD.

Appendix A:
Useful Information

1 If you need immediate support, use the telephone:

Parentline
Hayfa House, 57 Hart Road, Thundersley, Essex SS7 3PD. Tel: 01268 757007

Parent Network
44–46 Caversham Road, London NW5 2DS. Tel: 0171-485 8535

2 If you want to find a special school for your child in the UK, look in the following publications, which should be stocked by your local library:

Education Authorities Directory and Annual (Current Year)
The School Government Publishing Company, Darby House, Bletchingly Road, Mersham, Redhill, Surrey RH1 3DN.
ISBN 0 900640 31 6
ISBN 0 900640 32 4
ISSN 0070-9131

Special Schools in Britain (Current Year)
Network Publishing Ltd., Palmer House, Palmer Lane, Coventry, CV1 1FN.
ISBN 0 897759 02 9
ISSN 0968 1477

Which School? for Special Needs (Current Year)
John Catt Educational Ltd., Great Glemham, Saxmundham, Suffolk IP17 2DH.
ISBN 0 869863 25 9
ISSN 0965-10004

3   If you want to link up with support groups, find out more about difficult children, or discuss ADHD, the following associations will be able to help you:

United Kingdom
ADD Information Services
PO Box 340, Edgware, Middlesex HA8 9HL.

Association of Workers for Children with Emotional and Behavioural Difficulties
Charlton Court, East Sutton, Maidstone, Kent ME17 3DQ.

Hyperactive Children's Support Group
71 Whyke Lane, Chichester, West Sussex PO19 2LD.

Family Support Group UK
93 Avon Road, Devizes, Wiltshire SN10 1NT. Tel: Gill Mead 01373 826045. Brian Tuffil 01380 726710

London Support Group
88 Penhurst Gardens, Edgware, Middlesex HA8 9TU. Tel: Andrea Bilbow 0181 958 6727

Surrey Support Group
8 Broadwater Lane, Farncombe, Godalming, Surrey GU7 3JQ. Tel: Sharon Hawkins 01483 418398

Sussex Support Group
15 Harmans Mead, East Grinstead, West Sussex RH19 3XX. Tel: Linda Reimer 01342 311033

LADDER (Learning, Hyperactivity and Attention Disorders Association)
PO Box 700, Wolverhampton WV3 7YY.

Learning and Assessment Centre
Health Centre, Lower Tanbridge Way, Worthing Road, Horsham, West Sussex RH12 1JB. Tel: Dr G. D. Kewley 01403 240002. Fax: 01403 260900
(The Learning and Assessment Centre offers a fully comprehensive service involving educational psychology and paediatric assessment together with computerised continuous performance tests. It is regarded by many as the centre of ADD-ADHD expertise in the UK.)

United States:
Attention Deficit Disorder Association (ADDA)
PO Box 972, Mentor, OH 44061.

Adult ADHD Clinic
University of Massachusetts Medical Center, Department of Psychiatry, 55 Lake Avenue North, Worcester, MA 01655.

Children with Attention Deficit Disorders (CHADD)
499 Northwest 70th Avenue, Suite 308, Plantation, Florida 33317.

Canada
Canadian Paediatric Society
Centre hospitalier universitaire de Sherbrooke, Sherbrooke, Quebec J1H 5N4.

Society for Emotionally Disturbed Children
1622 Sherbrooke Street West, 3rd Floor, Montreal, Quebec H3H 1C9.

Australia
Active Hyperkinetic Children's Association
PO Box 17, East Doncaster, Victoria 3109.

Hyperactive Help (WA)
88 Manning Street, Scarborough WA 6019.

Launceston Hyperactivity Association
C/-PO, Meander, Tasmania 7304.

Queensland Hyperactivity Association
PO Box 107, Veronga, Queensland 3104.

New Zealand:
Auckland Hyperactivity Association
PO Box 36–099, Northcote, Auckland.

Waikato Hyperkinetic Children's Support Group
C/- 10 McFarlane Street, Hamilton.

Wellington Hyperactivity and Allergy Association, Inc.
93 Waipapa Road, Hataitai, Wellington.

4   If you want to read more about ADHD, here are just a few suggestions from the vast amount of available literature:

The ADD Hyperactivity Workbook for Parents, Teachers and Kids, H. Parker (1989), Impact Publications, Plantation, Florida, USA.

Managing Attention Disorders in Children: A guide for practitioners, S. Goldstein and M. Goldstein (1990), John Wiley & Sons, New York.

Your Hyperactive Child: A Parent's Guide to Coping with Attention Deficit Disorder, B. Ingersoll, Doubleday, New York.

The Hyperactive Child: A Parent's Guide, Professor Eric Taylor (1994), Optima.

The Hyperactive Child, Adolescent and Adult, Paul Wender (1987), Oxford University Press.

Chemical Cosh or Therapeutic Tool? Towards a balanced view of the use of stimulant medication with children diagnosed with Attention Deficit Hyperactivity Disorder, Katherine Ideus and Paul Cooper (1995), in *Therapeutic Care and Education*, 4, 3, 52–63.

These and many other publications, which can be used with young children, adolescents and adults who have ADHD, can be acquired through your local bookseller or from the following specialist distributors:

Being Yourself, 73 Liverpool Road, Deal, Kent CT14 7NN. Tel: 01304 381333

A.D.D. Warehouse, 300 NW 70th Avenue, Suite 102, Plantation, FL 33317, USA. Tel: 00 1 (305) 792-8944

Appendix B:
Code of Practice

If you are a parent of a child whose behaviour gives cause for concern, you should be aware of the Code of Practice which must now be adopted by all UK schools when a child is presenting difficulties.

Before going to see your child's teacher, it would be useful to read an outline of the various stages of identification and assessment of children who may have Special Educational Needs.

Whether you are a parent or a professional, you will find a wealth of useful information in relation to the Code of Practice in *Supporting Learning in the Primary School* by Alec Webster and Valerie Webster with Cliff Moon and Annie Warwick, Avec Designs Ltd., PO Box 709, Bristol BS99 1GE. The following extract is taken from this very helpful publication:

SUMMARY OF STAGES IN THE NEW CODE OF PRACTICE
Stage 1: gathering information, initial identification and registration of a child's SEN, and increased differentiation in the ordinary classroom
- responsibility for assessing children, differentiating teaching and devising appropriate plans remains with the class or subject teachers.
- trigger for Stage 1 is when a teacher, parent or other professional gives evidence of concern.
- class teacher must inform the headteacher, parents and SEN coordinator, who registers the child's SEN.
- parents' and child's own views on their difficulties must be sought.
- any known health or social problems are detailed, together with

profiles of achievement, National Curriculum Attainments and any other test data.
— class teacher can ask for help from school SEN coordinator, school doctor, other professional agency.
— support services (such as teacher of the deaf) can be called in from Stage 1 onwards, and always at Stage 3.
— record must be kept of nature of concern, action taken, targets set and when progress will be reviewed (within a term or six months, with parents kept informed).
— Stage 2 is reached if, after two reviews at Stage 1, special help has not resulted in satisfactory progress.

Stage 2: seeking further advice and/or the creation of an Individual Education Plan (IEP)

— school SEN coordinator takes the lead in assessing the child's learning difficulty, planning, monitoring and reviewing arrangements made.
— SEN coordinator seeks additional data from health, social services or other agencies and agrees appropriate action with parents and the child's teachers.
— IEP drawn up, setting out specific learning targets, using materials and resources within the normal classroom setting.
— IEP sets out nature of the child's difficulties, any special provision, staff involved including frequency of support, help from parents at home, targets to be achieved in a given time, monitoring and assessment arrangements, arrangements and date for review.
— parents should be invited to a review of Stage 2, which might take place within a term; talk to parents in person if considering moving a child to Stage 3.

Stage 3: school calls on outside specialist help

— responsibility for pupils with special needs is shared between the school SEN coordinator, class or subject teachers, and outside support services (such as visiting teachers or educational psychologists).
— new IEP drawn up including input from support services, detailing new targets and teaching strategies, monitoring and review arrangements.

- external agencies (such as teacher of visually impaired) may offer classroom support, advice on materials, technology or classroom management, or direct teaching.
- review organised by the SEN coordinator within a term, including parents, focusing on progress made, effectiveness of the IEP, any updated information and future plans.
- after review the headteacher considers referring the child to the LEA for a statutory assessment.
- LEA will require a range of written information and evidence to support the referral (educational and other developmental profiles, views of the parent and child, health and social factors).

Stage 4: statutory assessment
- needs of the great majority of children should be met under the first three Stages, with perhaps only 2 per cent of children being put forward for statementing.
- children may be brought to the LEA's attention for formal assessment by a number of routes, such as parental request, school referral or request from another agency.
- schools must demonstrate that child's needs remain so substantial that they cannot be met from the resources 'ordinarily available'.
- exceptionally, e.g. diagnosis of a major sensory impairment, may lead immediately to referral to the LEA for a multidisciplinary assessment.
- new Code sets out criteria for making statutory assessments, a timetable of 26 weeks for carrying out the whole process from start to finish, and the procedures which should be followed.
- local moderation groups may be set up to ensure consistency and fairness within an LEA.
- evidence required for statementing includes a wide spectrum of academic, social and emotional factors.

Stage 5: statementing
- statementing proceeds when LEA is satisfied that the child's needs are significant and/or complex; have not been met by measures taken by the school; or may call for resources which cannot 'reasonably be provided' within the budgets of mainstream schools in the area.

- statement is means of access to extra resources.
- provides a precise educational prescription for the child, based on an accurate and detailed account of needs.
- parental preferences must be taken into account and arrangements made for reviews.

Appendix C:
A Daily Record and Incident Sheet

If you are a parent or a professional it would be helpful to make notes on your child's behaviour. If you do this you may find that in actual fact he is behaving quite well, and that much of what he does is of no consequence. On the other hand, his behaviour might be much worse than you imagined. If this is the case then the notes will help you when you are discussing his problems with others. Rather than describing his behaviour in general terms you may be able usefully to observe a pattern from your notes.

NAME OF CHILD: DATE:

DATE OF BIRTH: HOME OR SCHOOL:

                    THIS RECORD COMPLETED BY:

                            Signed:......................

A   General Daily Record

HOME
Briefly comment on behaviour related to (a) staying on task, (b) being impulsive/hyperactive, when:

1   Playing with others:
2   Getting ready for school:
3   At mealtimes:
4   Having free time:
5   When visitors present:
6   Doing homework:
7   Getting ready for bed:
Other times when difficulties experienced:

SCHOOL
Briefly comment on behaviour related to (a) staying on task, (b) being impulsive/hyperactive, when:

1   Entering classroom:
2   During morning assembly:
3   Doing written assignments:
4   Doing practical assignments:
5   Working with others:
6   Working on own:
7   During breaktimes:
Other times when difficulties experienced:

B   Daily Incident Sheet (Home and School)

Use this part to analyse any incident which occurred today and caused you concern. (If there was none, make a note.)

Before the episode:
a   What was the child doing?
b   Were there any other children with him?
c   What were these others doing?
d   Was there an adult present?
e   Had a task been set for the child?
f   What measures had been taken to ensure that the task was appropriate for him?

During the episode:
a   Did anything specific occur to promote the crisis?
b   What actually happened in the incident?
c   Did the child physically attack 1) an adult or 2) a child?
d   Did the child use verbal abuse?
e   Did the child damage or use property when he lost control?
f   Did the child deliberately hurt himself?
g   Did the child appear completely out of control?
h   Did the action appear cold and premeditated?

Immediate resolution:
a   How was the situation resolved?

Appendices

b   Did a child or an adult resolve the situation?
c   How did they do this?
d   Did the child run off or resolve the situation himself?
e   What was the child's reaction afterwards?
f   How long did he take to calm down?

Final resolution:
a   If he talked to anyone later, who was this?
b   How did the child see the incident occurring?
c   Did he mention his ADHD and the part this might have played?
d   Was he full of remorse?
e   Was he keen to develop new strategies to avoid a recurrence?
f   What strategy was suggested?

Bibliography

American Psychiatric Association (1988). *Diagnostic and Statistical Manual of Mental Disorders* (DSM-111–R) (3rd edition revised), Washington, DC: APA.

American Psychiatric Association (1994). *Diagnostic and Statistical Manual of Mental Disorders* (DSM-IV), Washington, DC: APA.

Assagioli, R. (1975). *Psychosynthesis*, London: Turnstone Press.

Barkley, R. A. (1990). *Attention Deficit Hyperactivity Disorder: A handbook for diagnosis and treatment*, New York: Guilford Press.

Bettelheim, B. (1987). *The Good Enough Parent*, London: Thames & Hudson.

Campbell, S. B. (1990). *Behaviour Problems in Pre-school Children*, New York: Guilford Press.

Connors, C. K. (1989). *Connors Teacher Rating Scales*, Toronto: Multi-Health Systems.

Cooper, P. (1993). *Effective Schools for Disaffected Students*, London: Routledge.

Cooper, P. and Ideus, K. (1995). Attention Deficit Hyperactivity Disorder: Trojan Horse or Gift Horse? in *Attention Deficit/Hyperactivity Disorder: Educational, Medical and Cultural Issues*, Maidstone, Kent: AWCEBD.

Dupaul, G. J., Rapport, M. and Perriello, L. M. (1993). Does methylphenidate normalise the classroom performance of children with attention deficit disorder? in *Journal of the American Academy of Child and Adolescent Psychiatry*, 32, 190–198.

Feingold, B. F. (1995). *Why Your Child is Hyperactive*, New York: Random House.

Ferrucci, P. (1989). *What We May Be: the Vision and Techniques of Psychosynthesis*, London: Turnstone Press.

Garber, S. W., Garber, M. D. and Spizman R. F. (1993). *If Your Child is Hyperactive, Inattentive, Impulsive, Distractible*, New York: Villard Books.

Gelles, R. J. (1977). *Family Violence*, London: Sage Publications.

Gelles, R. J. (1987). *The Violent Home* (2nd edition), London: Sage Publications.

Gelles, R. J. (1985). *Intimate Violence in Families*, Beverly Hills: Sage Publications.

Goldstein, S. and Goldstein, M. (1990). *Managing Attention Disorders in Children: A Guide for Practitioners*, New York: John Wiley & Sons, Inc.

Gardner, A. (1987). *Hyperactivity, The So-Called Attention Deficit Disorder, and the Group of MBD Syndromes*, New Jersey: Creative Therapeutics.

Gulliford, R. and Upton, G. (1993). *Special Educational Needs*, London: DFE.

Hall, E. and Hall, C. (1988). *Human Relations in Education*, London: Routledge.

Halliwell, E. M. and Ratey, J. J. (1995). *Driven to Distraction: Recognising and Coping with Attention Deficit Disorder*, London and New York: Simon & Schuster.

Hendricks, G. (1977). *The Second Centering Book*, Englewood Cliffs, New York: Prentice Hall.

Hoghughi, M. (1988). *Treating Problem Children*, London: Sage Publications.

Hinshaw, S. (1994). *Attention Deficit Disorders and Hyperactivity in Children*, London: Sage Publications.

Kendall, P. C. and Braswell, L. (1985). *Cognitive-Behavioural Therapy for Impulsive Children*, New York: Guilford Press.

Kewley, G. (1995). Medical Aspects of Assessment and Treatment of Children with Attention Deficit Disorder, in *Attention Deficit/Hyperactivity Disorder: Educational, Medical and Cultural Issues*, Maidstone, Kent: AWCEBD.

Kirby, E. and Grimley, L. (1986). *Understanding and Treating Attention Deficit Disorder*, Oxford: Pergamon Press.

Laslett, R. (1977). *Educating Maladjusted Children*, London: Staples Press.

Mitchell, A. R. K. (1978). *Violence in the Family*, Hove, Sussex: Wayland Press.

O'Leary, D. (1984). *Mommy, I Can't Sit Still*, New York: New Horizon Press.

Parker, H. C. (1992). *The ADD Hyperactivity Handbook for Schools*, New York: Impact Publications.

Redl, F. and Wineman, D. (1965). *Controls from Within*. New York: Free Press.

Rhode, G., Jenson, W. R. and Reavis, H. K. (1992). *The Tough Kid Book: Practical Classroom Management Strategies*, CO: Sopris West, Inc.

Rogers, C. (1967). *On Becoming a Person*, London: Constable.

Rutter, M. (1975). *Helping Troubled Children*, Harmondsworth: Penguin Books.

Schachar, R. (1991). Childhood hyperactivity, in *Journal of Child Psychology and Psychiatry*, 32, 155–192.

Taylor, E. (1986). Childhood Hyperactivity, in *British Journal of Psychiatry*, 149, 562–573.

Taylor, E., Sandberg S., Thorley, G. and Giles, S. (1991). *The Epidemiology of Childhood Hyperactivity*, Maudsley Monographs No. 33, Oxford University Press.

Taylor, E. (1985). *The Hyperactive Child*, London: Optima.

Taylor, E. (1994). Hyperactivity as a special educational need, in *Therapeutic Care and Education*, 4, 2, 130–144.

Taylor, E. (1994). Syndromes of attention deficit and overactivity, in Rutter M., Taylor E. & Hersov L. (eds.), *Child and Adolescent Psychiatry: Modern Approaches* (3rd edition), Oxford: Blackwell Scientific Publications.

Train, A. G. (1993). *Helping the Aggressive Child*, London: Souvenir Press.

Walker, J. E. and Shea, T. M. (1991). *Behaviour Management: A practical approach for educators*, New York: Merrill Publishers.

Wedge, P. and Essen, J. (1973). *Born to Fail*, London: Arrow Books.

Wedge, P. and Essen, J. (1983). *Children in Adversity*, London: Pan Books.

Weiss, G. and Hechtman, L. T. (1986). *Hyperactive Children Grown Up*, New York: Guilford Press.

Wheldall, K. and Glynn, T. (1989). *Effective Classroom Learning*, Oxford: Blackwell.

Index